The
Duck
COOKBOOK

The Duck
COOKBOOK

JAMES PETERSON

Stewart, Tabori & Chang
New York

Page ii: Slow-Roasted Duck Legs with Sauerkraut.

Published in 2003 by
Stewart, Tabori & Chang
A Company of La Martinière Groupe
115 West 18th Street
New York, NY 10011

Export Sales to all countries except Canada, France, and French-speaking Switzerland:
Thames and Hudson Ltd.
181A High Holborn
London WC1V 7QX
England

Canadian Distribution:
Canadian Manda Group
One Atlantic Avenue, Suite 105
Toronto, Ontario M6K 3E7
Canada

Library of Congress Cataloging-in-Publication Data

Peterson, James.
    The duck cookbook / James Peterson.
    ISBN 1-58479-295-7
    1. Cookery (Duck) I. Title.

TX750.5.D82P43 2003
641.6'6597—dc21   2003045850

DESIGN BY Nina Barnett
The text of this book was composed in Bembo and Frutiger.

Printed in Hong Kong

10 9 8 7 6 5 4 3 2 1

First Printing

Acknowledgments

I am very fortunate to be surrounded by a core of supportive people who help me in myriad ways with my various books and projects. I've been fortunate to work with many of you before and hope to continue to do so.

When compiling a cookbook, little if anything is more important than the certainty that the recipes do what they say they'll do. For this, I have to thank my recipe tester, Stephanie Shapiro, whose careful attention to detail and ability to spot ambiguities and contradictions have been invaluable. She also helped proofread many of the recipes and came up with some ideas of her own. Her hands also appear in the how-to photographs.

Since there are a great number of recipes in this book, the work of food stylist Ann Disrude, and her magical ability to make virtually anything look appetizing, has been especially important. Her assistant Mark Ibold was a great help, too, and brought conviviality to the sometimes rather arduous days of shooting. Many thanks to Debre DeMers, photo assistant and close friend, for her eye for detail, her efficiency, and for keeping us all laughing.

I am indeed indebted to the team at Stewart, Tabori & Chang. They have always been encouraging and shown ongoing appreciation for my work. My publisher and editor, Leslie Stoker, is a joy to work with, and freelance editor Sarah Scheffel has been beyond conscientious, helping me with the countless details involved in preparing the manuscript and layouts in their various metamorphoses. She has been my partner in the continuous struggle against chaos. My thanks also to the truly talented designer Nina Barnett, and the diligent proofreader Ana Deboo.

Then there are those who've been with me from the beginning. My agents Elise and Arnold Goodman deserve high praise for always making themselves available and for listening to my whining when things aren't going quite the way I want them to. They continue to work very hard for me. And as always, thanks to my partner and food guinea pig, Zelik, for appreciating me and what I do, and for his constant encouragement.

Contents

Introduction

While it may seem odd to write a whole book about a single bird, the versatile and flavorful duck deserves this special attention. As you will discover, you can make duck into sausages, salamis, prosciutto, pastrami, and other smoked dishes, or it can be stewed, slow-baked, or used as a component in a wide variety of salads. You can steam, braise, or sauté it, and accompany it with dozens of different sauces, or turn it into that rich and satisfying French specialty, confit. You can serve it hot, cold, rare, or cooked all day.

No doubt because the prospect of cooking duck intimidates people, I've never been served it in someone's home. This is a pity, since duck is a perfect compromise between chicken and red meat and never fails to delight guests. If you learn to cook duck in just one of the dozens of ways described in this book—from the simple to the complex—you'll be able to make spectacular guest fare that requires as little or as much effort as you like. While you may choose to use the large breasts taken from special ducks known as mullards, it is also possible to make luxurious dishes with ordinary frozen Pekin (also called Long Island) ducklings sold in supermarkets.

When confronted with a whole duck, most of us think we should roast it as though it were a chicken. Because most of the ducks available in the United States have thick, very fatty skin, the results of our roasting efforts can be mediocre or worse. If a Pekin duck is cooked long enough to give up its fat and turn crispy on the outside, the meat inside is *very* well done. This isn't necessarily bad, but it's limiting when you consider all of duck's possibilities. If you cook the whole duck until the meat is rosy pink—a nice medium rare—the skin will be flabby and greasy and, well, dreadful.

LEFT: *Duck prosciutto (recipe on page 101) with fresh fruit.*

Duck has a lot of flavor, and if the skin is removed it's very lean—leaner and much tastier than a skinless chicken breast. If you're cooking duck for the first time, instead of grappling with the whole duck, I suggest you cook just the breasts, which are often sold by themselves nowadays. If you do end up buying a whole duck and want to remove the breasts, cut up the carcass as shown on pages 5 to 6 and freeze the parts you don't use. Every bit of a duck can be eaten except the bones, and these can be simmered to make a flavorful broth that can in turn be used to make soups, sauces, and stews. Sauté the breasts following the basic recipe on page 14 and you'll have made your first duck dinner in just 15 minutes.

Because of its idiosyncrasies, particularly its fatty skin, duck must be approached differently than any other meat, poultry or otherwise. The secret to cooking a duck is to cook each of its parts in a different way. Because duck breast meat is very lean, it mustn't be overcooked or it will dry out. It has to be sautéed so that the fat in the skin renders before the meat overcooks. When done right—and it's hard to do it wrong—a sautéed duck breast is crispy and juicy at the same time. Duck legs are an entirely different matter. If you simply sauté or grill a duck leg, it will be tough, plus I think there's something unappealing about rare or medium-rare duck-leg meat. Duck legs are best when they are slowly braised with a little wine or homemade duck broth or when they are made into a confit, which involves gently simmering the legs in duck fat that you've trimmed off other parts of the duck. Duck legs are also good slow-roasted, which makes the fat crispy and the flesh meltingly tender.

Combining techniques is another option. You can gently stew the duck's legs until they're soft and juicy, then finish them on the grill; or you can pat them with cornstarch or dip them in batter and then deep-fry them (see page 95) until you have a crispy crust surrounding meat that's more reminiscent of a well-made stew than of something fried. You can make confit and grill or smoke the already-tender meat, or shred the confit to create rillettes, which, when smeared and toasted, might be the best spread in existence. You can turn the braising liquid from the duck legs into a sauce, flavor it however you like, and serve it over the cooked legs or sautéed duck breasts.

Virtually all the classic French dishes for whole roasted duck can be made from sautéed duck breasts or from braised or slow-roasted legs instead. Consider duck à l'orange. In most French cookbooks, the recipe calls for roasting a whole duck—French ducks don't have the thick, fatty skin that ours do—then the duck's juices are combined with orange juice and orange zest cut into minute strips, and the mixture is simmered to reduce it, then thickened with a little cornstarch. If you follow this method, the only thing orange about the duck is the sauce. But

Fresh versus Frozen

In many parts of the country, the only ducks available are frozen Pekin ducks (sometimes called Long Island ducklings). Fortunately duck freezes well and can even stand being frozen twice. If you make a recipe calling only for duck thighs, just refreeze the breasts by wrapping them tightly in plastic wrap and then in aluminum foil to prevent freezer burn. Sometimes Pekin ducks can be found fresh—they usually need to be preordered—but the difference they offer is so minor, I usually don't bother. (Frozen breasts cook quickly, from rare to medium, when sautéed or grilled.)

the simplest thing is to replace the duck's juices with concentrated duck or chicken broth and the whole duck with sautéed duck breasts. Or you can braise duck legs and use the braising liquid as the base for the orange sauce, then sauté the breasts and top both the leg meat and the breasts with the sauce. For grilled duck à l'orange, try grilling or smoking duck breasts, brushing them as they cook with an orange juice and orange zest glaze. (See page 18 for recipe.)

Duck is versatile not only in that it lends itself to all sorts of cooking techniques, but in the many ways it can be presented and served. It's not so expensive that it need be thought of as a luxury food, but it can be treated as something very special. If you want to be extrava-

ABOVE: *Duck, Cabbage, and Borlotti Bean* Potée *(recipe on page 117).*

gant, serve duck breasts topped with kitchen delicacies such as truffles and wild mushrooms. They can also be served with a wide variety of sauces to create effects ranging from rustic—duck confit with spinach (see page 78)—to elegant and cosmopolitan—a sautéed duck breast with a slab of foie gras on top (see page 25). And if you don't want to make any extra effort, sautéed duck breasts are good with no sauce at all.

VARIETIES OF DUCK

There are so many species of ducks (scores of them) and hybrids made by crossing one breed with another, it's almost impossible to trace the lineage of the ducks we eat. It seems, however, that all domestic ducks are descendants of one of two species, the mallard and the muscovy duck. The mallard is a common wild duck—the male is easily identified by its metallic green head and neck—and, when shot in the wild, has a delicious flavor. I've tasted domesticated mallards but found them tough and lacking the flavor of their wild relatives.

Muscovy ducks originated in South America and are a different species entirely. Much of what I've read says these ducks have a strong musky flavor, but in my experience they've been full-flavored and leaner than most domesticated ducks but somewhat tough. They are crossbred with other duck species to create some of the varieties enjoyed around the world today. In France muscovy ducks are bred with Rouen or Nantes ducks (both descendants of mallards) to create Barbary ducks, the domesticated variety most often found in that country. They are much like our Long Island ducklings except meatier, with less fatty skin, so when they are roasted whole the skin gets crispy while the meat stays rare to medium rare. Rouen ducks are best known as the duck used to make the French specialty pressed duck; unfortunately they're not available in the United States.

It's hard to know where wild ducks originated, since they're migratory birds and their remains can be found all over the world, but ducks were probably first domesticated in China, possibly as early as 3000 B.C. Eventually Chinese domesticated ducks evolved into what we now call Pekin (why not Peking I have no idea) or Long Island ducklings. (The words "duck" and "duckling" can be used interchangeably because most ducks are sold while they are still young and tender.) These have a characteristic thick and fatty skin and a lovely flavor.

Unless you're a hunter or have a hunter friend, you'll generally have access to only two varieties of duck: the Pekin or Long Island duck, found frozen at the supermarket (fortunately duck freezes well), and mullard ducks, which are rarely seen whole but whose giant breasts (a pound or more) are sold fresh or frozen on their own. Mullards are created by crossing muscovy ducks with mallards. Since you can buy the breasts alone, mullards are convenient, and they are delicious, with a gamier flavor than Pekin ducks. The breasts are so meaty, you can serve them as you would a steak. Mullard breasts are more likely to be encountered fresh, sealed in Cryovac. Until recently, mullard breasts were the only breasts you could buy alone, without getting the whole duck. Some markets are beginning to sell breasts and thighs separately so you're not stuck with one when cooking the other. In France any duck breasts taken off the bone can be labeled a *magret,* whereas in the United States a *magret* is specifically a breast from a mullard.

I tasted my first duck, a mallard shot by my father and roasted to a perfect medium rare by my mother, when I was seven years old. I knew immediately and without doubt that it was the most delicious thing I had ever tasted. Oddly, that duck's flavor was familiar—almost as though I remembered it from a past life—even though I was certain I had never tasted anything like it before. Since then, truffles are the only other food to evoke such strange and semiconscious associations.

If you're lucky enough to get a hold of a mallard and want to recreate my childhood experience, simply roast it in a 450°F oven, brushed once or twice with melted butter, until the breast meat is rare to medium rare, usually about 25 minutes. The thighs are tough and scrawny and not worth bothering with, unless perhaps you want to concoct a little sauce or jus. While my first duck was a wild one, with a flavor that's impossible to extract from a domesticated duck, even the most "ordinary" frozen supermarket duck, when lovingly and knowingly prepared, can come amazingly close.

HOW TO CUT UP A WHOLE DUCK

Every part of a duck is useful, not just the legs and the breasts. Use the wings and bones for broth, and the fat for confit or as an all-purpose cooking fat—it's marvelous for omelets. Tightly wrap the parts you don't use in plastic wrap and stick them in the freezer, where they will keep for months. If the duck is frozen, leave it in the refrigerator for a day or two—put it in a bowl because it releases juices—or leave it out at cool room temperature for a day. If you're in a rush, soak it in room-temperature water, changing the water every 15 minutes. To cut up a duck, start with the breast side down on a cutting board.

1. Cut off the flap of skin that's attached to one end of the duck. Save it for making confit.

2. With the breast side down, cut off the wings where they join the body.

3. Cut under and around the joints to detach the wings.

4. Cut through the skin along the edge of one leg, turning the duck over as you go.

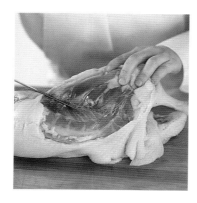

5. When you've cut down to the back, start cutting away the leg.

6. Keeping the knife flush against the back, continue cutting away the leg.

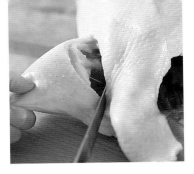

7. Continue until you completely detach the leg.

8. Turn the duck around to take the leg off the other side.

9. Continue cutting through the skin to detach the thigh. Bend the thigh all the way back until the joint pops out.

10. Continue sliding the knife flush against the back until you remove the leg.

11. Turn the duck breast side up. Slide a sharp knife along one side of the cartilaginous bone that runs between breasts.

12. Cut the breast away along the entire length of the duck.

13. Peel the breast back while cutting between the meat and breastbone.

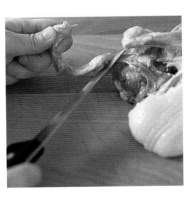

14. Cut under the wishbone, detaching it from the breast meat.

15. Keeping the knife flush against the carcass, cut away the breast. Cut away the fat surrounding the breast.

16. Cut around the wishbone and remove it.

17. Cut away the other breast and remove its excess fat.

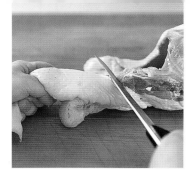

18. Pull away the breast with its surrounding fat.

19. Cut off the tail. Cut off the skin and fat from the carcass and reserve.

20. Hold the carcass on one end. Hack through it with a cleaver, separating the back and rib cage.

21. Break the back into 3 or 4 pieces and the breastbone into 2 pieces.

22. Cut the wings into 3 pieces for broth.

USING EVERY PART OF THE DUCK: DUCK FAT

Pekin and mullard ducks are covered with a thick layer of fatty skin. When gently rendered, it produces clear, white fat that congeals when cold but is clear and liquid when heated. Duck fat also happens to be delicious.

To render duck fat, save the skin from raw ducks—I save it in the freezer, tightly wrapped, until I have enough to make a project out of it, but it's worth saving even the skin from one duck carcass—and chop it fine, either by hand or in a food processor. Put it in a heavy-bottomed pot and cook it over medium heat until clear. When small pieces of skin left in the fat begin to turn brown and the fat itself is perfectly clear, usually after 1 to 2 hours, depending on the quantity, it's ready to strain. (Be very careful not to overcook the fat or it will lose its flavor. It's better to err in the direction of undercooking.) Strain the fat into containers with tight-fitting lids (I use containers saved from take-out food), let it cool, and refrigerate for a month or two or freeze it indefinitely. (For directions on saving the fat that duck breasts render during sautéing, see page 15).

Duck Broth

*A*mong duck's many attributes are its versatility and the fact that you can use every part of it: the breasts for sautéing; the thighs for braising, grilling, and frying; the wings and bones for making broth. When making duck broth, figure you'll get slightly less than 1 quart of broth per duck carcass. If you want concentrated broth, you'll obtain about 1 cup per carcass. When making a duck glaze—great as a base for sauces—you'll get just ¼ cup per carcass. If you simmer the carcass in chicken or duck broth instead of water, you'll end up with broth that's twice as concentrated—about 2 cups concentrated broth or ½ cup glaze per carcass. This recipe calls for twelve duck carcasses and makes lots of broth. Feel free to adjust the quantities to suit your needs.

MAKES ABOUT 9 QUARTS

12 duck carcasses and leftover pieces such as wings
3 large onions, peeled and chopped coarse
3 carrots, peeled and cut into 1-inch pieces
12 quarts brown chicken broth (see page 10) or water, or more as needed
1 bouquet garni (1 small bunch parsley, about 7 sprigs fresh thyme or
*   1 teaspoon dried thyme, and 2 imported bay leaves, tied together with*
*   kitchen twine or wrapped in cheesecloth)*

BELOW, LEFT TO RIGHT: *1. Spread chopped up duck parts and vegetables in roasting pan. 2. Roast until well browned. 3. Transfer roasted ingredients to pot and add liquid to pan. Put pan on stovetop and scrape up any caramelized juices. 4. Add deglazing liquid to pot with enough water or broth to cover.*

To make brown duck broth: Preheat the oven to 500°F. Coarsely chop the duck carcasses and any spare duck bones with a cleaver or heavy chefs' knife. Brown them in a roasting pan with the onions and carrots for 1 hour, stirring after about 30 minutes. Transfer the browned carcasses and vegetables to a stockpot, and add about 1 quart of the broth or water to the roasting pan, scraping up bits of caramelized juice with a wooden spoon.

To the stockpot, add the bouquet garni, the liquid you used to deglaze the roasting pan, and enough chicken broth or water to cover—about 11 quarts. Simmer gently over low heat for at least 6 hours or overnight—you can't simmer the bones too long, but the broth should never reach a full boil. Set the pot slightly off-center on the heat source so the broth simmers on one side only. This pushes the fat and scum to the other side, which makes them easier to skim off. Use a ladle, held so the bowl is almost perfectly flat, to skim off the fat and froth every 30 minutes; this is especially important near the beginning. Add water or broth during simmering if needed to keep the bones covered.

When the broth is done, remove the bouquet garni and strain the broth through a coarse-mesh strainer or, better yet, a "china cap," a sheet-metal strainer shaped like a cone. The idea is to choose a strainer that you can use some force on without damaging. Brown duck broth will keep for a week in the refrigerator.

To make concentrated duck broth: Simmer the 9 quarts brown duck broth until it's reduced to about one fourth the volume—that's 9 cups—skimming off fat and froth as you go. (Or if you used broth instead of water to make the brown duck broth, reduce to just 4½ quarts.) Strain the concentrated broth through a fine-mesh strainer to finish. Concentrated broth will keep for a week in the refrigerator.

To make duck glaze: The French call this *glace de canard,* and it is handy for throwing together quick sauces. To make it, reduce 9 cups concentrated broth down to 2 cups (or the 4½ quarts down to 4 cups) and strain the glaze through a fine-mesh strainer. Duck glaze will keep for a week or longer in the refrigerator.

Duck glaze and veal glaze, both of which can be used for making duck sauces and stews, are also available commercially. More-than-Gourmet (see Sources, page 154) manufactures a variety of good concentrated stocks and glazes. The three that I find most useful when making duck dishes are Glace de Canard Gold (duck glaze), Demi-Glace Gold (veal glaze lightly thickened with flour), and Glace de Viande Gold (veal glaze). Because they are very concentrated, all of these commercial glazes should be used in very small amounts, about half as much as the homemade glaze described above. When using your own homemade glaze, keep in mind that there may be variations in concentration between one batch and another. Because of this, you may need to reduce your sauce to thicken it, or thin it with a little broth or water to get it to the consistency you like.

Duck Broth and Glaze Equivalents

When making sauces for sautéed duck breasts, you can use broth, concentrated broth, the braising liquid from duck legs, or glaze, each in varying amounts depending on their concentration. Approximate equivalents, to be used for the recipes in this book, are supplied below.

Since it's impossible to give exact amounts for each of these ingredients, keep in mind that a sauce base—the liquid in the pan after you've added the broth or glaze but before you've added butter or cream—may need to be thickened or thinned. To thicken the base, simply boil it until it has the consistency you like; to thin it, simply add a little more broth or water.

4 quarts brown duck broth made with water = 1 quart concentrated duck broth = 1 cup homemade duck glaze = ½ cup commercial glaze such as Demi-Glace Gold

4 quarts brown duck broth made with broth = 2 quarts concentrated duck broth = 2 cups homemade duck glaze = 1 cup commercial glaze such as Demi-Glace Gold

Concentrated Brown Chicken Broth

Chicken broth is useful if you're making a base for a duck sauce but don't have any duck parts except the breasts. You can also use chicken broth to moisten duck parts to make duck broth that is half as concentrated as the concentrated broth described on page 9. This chicken broth is already very concentrated, flavorful, and almost as clear as consommé (clarified broth). The trick is to cook the chicken parts first in the oven so their juices caramelize and contribute color and flavor to the broth. By cooking the chicken before adding liquid, you also cause the proteins in the chicken to coagulate inside the meat instead of in the broth, so the broth is clear rather than cloudy.

MAKES 2½ QUARTS

6 pounds chicken wings, drumsticks, thighs, or backs
   (break the backs into at least 3 pieces each with a cleaver)
1 large onion, root end cut off, quartered from top to bottom without peeling
3 medium carrots, greens removed, scrubbed but not peeled,
   halved lengthwise and sliced
1 stalk celery, sliced (optional)
1 handful fennel stalks (optional)
1 bouquet garni (3 sprigs thyme, 3 sprigs parsley, and 1 imported bay leaf,
   tied together with kitchen twine)

Spread the chicken parts, onion, and carrots, along with the celery and fennel if you're using them, in a heavy-bottomed roasting pan just large enough to hold them in a single layer. (If the pan is too large, the juices will burn; if it's too small, the chicken won't brown properly.)

Slide the pan into the oven, turn the temperature to 400°F—since there's no need for preheating, you might as well save a little gas—and bake for 1 to 1½ hours, stirring the vegetables and chicken a couple of times during the baking so they brown evenly and thoroughly. From time to time, tilt the roasting pan and spoon out and discard excess fat. Don't, however, acci-

dentally discard any uncaramelized juices that may be underneath the liquid fat.

When the chicken and vegetables are well browned and the bottom of the roasting pan is covered with a golden-brown glaze, take the pan out of the oven and place it on the stovetop. If the chicken and vegetables have browned but there's a cloudy liquid on the bottom of the pan (perfectly clear liquid is rendered fat), turn the heat to high and stir the chicken pieces around until any liquid—except fat—caramelizes into a glaze at the bottom of the pan. Tilt the pan and spoon out any more transparent liquid fat.

Pour 1 quart water into the roasting pan and, over high heat, scrape the bottom of the pan with a wooden spoon until the water comes to a simmer and the glaze dissolves, about 5 minutes. Scrape everything out of the roasting pan into a heavy-bottomed pot. Ideally, the pot should be narrow and tall so the fat and foam will be contained in a smaller area, making it easier to skim. Nestle in the bouquet garni and pour in enough cold water to cover the chicken parts by about 1 inch.

Bring to a simmer, but not a boil, over high heat. Turn down the heat to maintain at a murmur—a bubble rising every second or two—with the pot set slightly off-center on the burner. This pushes the fat and foam to one side, also making it easier to skim. Simmer for about 2 hours, adding an additional 2 cups broth or water to keep the chicken covered. Strain, let cool, and refrigerate. When the broth has gelled, spoon off and discard any congealed fat from its surface if you're using the broth right way. Otherwise, leave the layer of concentrated fat until you're ready to use the broth—it helps to preserve it. Broth should keep in the refrigerator for a week—if you want to keep it longer, spoon off the congealed fat and simmer the refrigerated broth for 5 minutes, let it cool again, and it will last another week—and for a year in the freezer.

HOW MUCH DUCK TO SERVE?

People's appetites vary so much that it's hard to give exact serving amounts, especially when duck legs are on the menu. If you're serving just breasts, a whole breast from a Long Island duckling (Pekin duck) is just right for a single main-course serving. If you're serving mullard breasts, half a breast per person is about right. If you're serving the legs, one leg alone can serve one, but it's a bit of a stretch, especially if your guests are big eaters and you haven't served a first course. Two legs, on the other hand, is usually too much. I sometimes resolve this problem by dividing the legs into thighs and drumsticks and giving everyone two of one and one of the other. You can also serve duck legs and breasts together: Serve half a sliced mullard breast with a whole duck leg; or serve most or all of a Pekin duck breast with a duck leg to produce a generous main-course serving.

Sautéing

MOST OF THE TIME, sautéing means cooking in a frying pan over high heat with a little bit of fat in the pan to prevent sticking. High heat is used so that a tasty crust forms on the outside of whatever it is—meat, fish, or vegetable—that you're sautéing. Because most foods release liquid as they cook, high heat is needed to get the liquid to evaporate the instant it's released. That way the liquid helps form a crust on the food instead of just running out into the pan and causing the food to steam.

If you're sautéing a steak, chop, or fish fillet, you'll need to adjust the temperature of the pan based on the meat or fillet's thickness. Duck breasts have their own requirements. If you're sautéing a skinless duck breast, you'll need very high heat to brown the meat while leaving it rare to medium rare on the inside. Like a steak or other red meats, it should only reach an internal temperature of about 125°F. This is unlike a chicken breast, which can spend enough time in the pan to brown and cook through, meaning that you can cook it over medium heat until it reaches an internal temperature of about 140°F.

If you're sautéing a skin-on duck breast, which is far tastier than a skinless breast, you'll want to get the fatty skin side of the breast to render its fat and turn crispy without overcooking the meat. There are a couple of tricks that help accomplish this. One is to make a series of crisscrossing slashes in the duck skin—see the photo opposite—so that the skin will render its fat more quickly. Another is to cook the breast almost entirely skin side down and then sauté it for just a minute or so on the fleshy side.

When sautéing with the skin side down, check during the cooking—which takes 8 to 10 minutes for Pekin duck breasts and 12 to 18 minutes for mullards—to make sure the skin is browning at the right speed. If after 2 minutes the breast is already brown, turn down the heat; if after 5 minutes it's still pale and flabby, increase the heat. (Think of it like bacon: If you put it in a smoking-hot pan, it will burn on the outside yet stay raw and flabby inside.) When the skin turns medium to dark brown and the breast just begins to feel firm to the touch, ideally after the requisite cooking times described above, turn the breast over and cook Pekin duck breasts for 1 minute on the fleshy side and mullard breasts for 2 minutes.

Sautéed Duck Breasts

MAKES 4 MAIN-COURSE SERVINGS

4 Pekin (Long Island) duck breasts
or 2 mullard breasts (1½ to 2 pounds total)
Salt and pepper

Use a long, thin, and very sharp knife to cut about 20 slashes into the skin of each duck breast (see photo, page 12). Cut deep, but not deep enough to expose the meat—leaning the knife to the side somewhat will help cut through as much fat as possible. Give the breast a 90-degree turn and cut 20 more slashes to intersect the ones you made first. Season with salt and pepper.

Heat a sauté pan over medium to high heat—you don't need any fat since the duck will release its own—and sauté the breasts, skin side down, 8 to 10 minutes for the Pekin duck breasts and 12 to 18 minutes for the mul-lard. Turn the breasts over to the fleshy side, adjust the heat to high, and sauté for 1 minute for the Pekin duck and 2 minutes for the mullard. You can tell when the breasts are done by pressing firmly on one with your finger. When underdone, it will feel soft and fleshy, but when done, the meat will begin to bounce back to the touch. This takes a little practice, but once you get it, you'll never need a clock or thermometer again.

While holding each breast down with a fork, slice it crosswise with a sharp knife held at an angle. Serve immediately.

CLASSIC FRENCH SAUCES FOR SAUTÉED DUCK BREASTS

Many of us avoid making a classic French sauce because we don't have any homemade broth to base it on. There are a couple of ways around this. The first is to just leave the broth out. The sauce won't have the same depth of flavor, but there are plenty of delicious liquids—from fortified wines such as port or Madeira or Muscat de Beaumes de Venise, to red or white wines, to orange juice—that you can add to the pan to dissolve the caramelized liquids and produce an acceptable sauce or glaze. (See Reducing and Degreasing, page 43).

If you do want to use broth or, better yet, concentrated broth to deglaze your pan, you have several options. You can buy ready-made concentrated broth at most gourmet stores, you can make a duck broth from duck carcasses and simmer it down to concentrate it, or you can braise duck legs (see page 36) and use the braising liquid as the base for your sauce. A good homemade brown chicken broth is also an option. See page 8 for more about broths, concentrated broths, and glazes.

Sautéed Duck Breasts with Wild Mushrooms

MAKES 4 MAIN-COURSE SERVINGS

4 Pekin (Long Island) duck breasts or 2 mullard breasts (1½ to 2 pounds total)
Salt and pepper
1 to 1½ pounds wild mushrooms, such as chanterelles, morels, porcini, or hedgehogs,
*   alone or in combination, rinsed and patted dry (some mushrooms, like porcinis*
*   and morels, cook down more than others)*

Score, season, and sauté the breasts according to the directions on page 14. Be sure that the breasts fit snugly in the pan in a single layer—if the inside of the pan is exposed, the fat will accumulate in that area and burn. Transfer the breasts to a plate and keep warm. Turn the heat to high and immediately add the mushrooms to the pan. Sauté them for about 5 min-utes, until they smell fragrant and any water they release has evaporated.

Slice the breasts crosswise, arrange the slices on individual heated plates, spoon the mushrooms over them, and serve.

HOW TO SAVE THE RENDERED FAT

There's no denying that duck fat is not only very tasty, it's very useful in the kitchen for browning meats or seafood, for sautéing potatoes and other vegetables, and perhaps best of all, for making omelets. If you're careful, you can save the fat that duck breasts render as they sauté. First you must sauté the breasts in a heavy-bottomed pan just large enough to hold them in a single layer. If the pan is too big, the fat will spread into the empty areas and burn. You can judge if you burned the fat by its smell, which should be like duck, not burned fat. (Again, think of bacon, which behaves in much the same way: You can smell it when bacon fat has burned even if the bacon slices themselves have not.) You can save some of the fat by pouring it out of the sauté pan after about 5 minutes and discarding the fat that's released after that. After just 5 minutes, the fat won't have had time to burn.

Duck with Blueberries

*D*uck with black currants is a classic French dish, but since those fresh berries are almost impossible to find, I use blueberries. The small wild blueberries that are in season in early summer are best, but if you can't find them, just use the big kind. The principles behind making duck with blueberries are the same as for duck à l'orange (see page 18), or for that matter, duck with any fruit. The duck breasts are sautéed, then the pan is deglazed with either the fruit's juice (impractical for blueberries) or a sweet wine, such as port or Madeira. The fruit is added, its flavor enhanced with sugar and vinegar, and the sauce is finished with a little butter.

Any fruit can be substituted if you use a bit of commonsense: Peaches or apricots must be peeled, cut into wedges, and lightly cooked in butter before adding them to the sauce with any juices they've released; for raspberries, the recipe is identical to the blueberry treatment below; and figs must be roasted with butter and sugar, then served next to the duck on the plate.

4 Pekin (Long Island) duck breasts or 2 mullard breasts (1½ to 2 pounds total)
Salt and pepper
1 cup blueberries (preferably the small wild variety), raspberries, or blackberries
½ cup port or ¼ cup water
1 cup concentrated duck broth, ¼ cup homemade duck glaze,
*   or 2 tablespoons commercial glaze (see pages 8 to 11 and Note)*
1 tablespoon raspberry, sherry, or red wine vinegar, or more to taste
2 tablespoons cold unsalted butter

Use a sharp knife to score the skin side of the duck breasts in two directions, about 20 slashes per direction (see page 14 for more detailed instructions). Season the breasts on both sides with salt and pepper. Reserve in the refrigerator.

Rinse the blueberries and put them in a saucepan with the port or water. Cover the pan and cook for 5 minutes over medium heat and then for 10 minutes more, uncovered, to concentrate the juices released by the berries. In the meantime, if you're using concentrated duck broth, reduce it in another saucepan to about ¼ cup to turn it into a glaze. Add the glaze to the blueberries and their juices, stir to combine, and boil the sauce for a minute or two, until it has a very light, syrupy consistency. Whisk in the vinegar and butter, and season to taste with salt. (The sauce can be made several hours before serving, except the butter must be added to the simmering sauce at the end.)

Heat a sauté pan over medium to high heat and sauté the duck breasts, skin side down, 8 to 10 minutes for the Pekin duck breasts and 12 to 18 minutes for the mullard. Turn the breasts over, adjust the heat to high, and cook for 1 minute for the Pekin duck and 2 minutes for the mullard.

Slice the breasts crosswise, arrange the slices on individual heated plates, spoon the sauce over the breasts, and serve.

NOTE: If you've braised duck legs recently, you can substitute 1½ cups braising liquid cooked down to ½ cup first.

LEFT: *Duck with Blueberries, shown here with asparagus spears and slices of blue Peruvian potatoes.*

Duck à l'Orange

*W*hile it may sound like a cliché, duck has a natural affinity for oranges and, for that matter, for most things sweet. Traditional recipes for duck à l'orange call for bitter Seville oranges that provide just the right note of dissonance to match their sweetness. When I can't find them—which is most of the time—I look for kumquats; if I can't find kumquats, I just use a regular juicing orange. The Grand Marnier also adds a hint of bitter orange.

To make duck à l'orange—or duck à la kumquat—you'll need duck glaze, either your own or store-bought. If you want to use duck legs too (see the variation on page 20), you can use the liquid from braising the duck legs. Making duck à l'orange is a useful project because once you understand how it's made, you can improvise virtually any French duck sauce using the same method.

MAKES 4 MAIN-COURSE SERVINGS

4 Pekin (Long Island) duck breasts or 2 mullard breasts (1½ to 2 pounds total)
Salt and pepper
12 kumquats or 1 juicing orange
1 cup water
1 cup concentrated duck broth, ¼ cup homemade duck glaze,
  or 2 tablespoons commercial glaze (see pages 8 to 9)
¾ teaspoon sugar
2 tablespoons Grand Marnier
2 tablespoons balsamic, sherry, or red wine vinegar, or more to taste
3 tablespoons cold unsalted butter
Orange wedges (optional; see Cutting Perfect Orange Wedges, page 20)

Use a sharp knife to score the skin side of the duck breasts in two directions, about 20 slashes per direction (see page 14 for more detailed instructions). Season the breasts on both sides with salt and pepper. Reserve in the refrigerator.

Cut the round ends off the kumquats and eat or discard them. Set the kumquats on one end and use a sharp paring knife to trim the zests off six of them. Cut all the kumquats in half lengthwise, and working over a strainer set in a nonreactive bowl, remove the pulp with a small spoon. Push the pulp against the strainer to extract the juice. (Don't worry if you end up with only a tablespoon or two.) Place the kumquat zests on a cutting board and slice them into fine julienne. Bring the 1 cup water to a boil over high heat, blanch the zests for 1 minute, then drain them in a strainer.

If you're using the orange instead, cut off one end so the orange can stand on the cutting board, and slice off four 2-inch strips of zest. Cut the zest into fine julienne, then blanch the zest for 1 minute in the cup of boiling water. Juice the orange, strain the juice into a saucepan, and boil it until it's reduced to about 2 tablespoons.

If you're using concentrated duck broth, reduce it in a small saucepan to about ¼ cup—until it's lightly syrupy.

Heat a sauté pan over medium to high heat and sauté the duck breasts, skin side down, 8 to 10 minutes for the Pekin duck breasts and 12 to 18 minutes for the mullard. Turn the breasts over, adjust the heat to high, and cook for 1 minute for the Pekin ducks and 2 minutes for the mullard.

Pour the fat out of the pan—if it hasn't burned, save it for omelets—and deglaze the pan with the reduced kumquat or orange juice. Use a whisk to add the glaze. Add the sugar, Grand Marnier, kumquat or orange zest, and vinegar, and simmer the sauce for about 30 seconds to cook off the alcohol. At this point, adjust the thickness of the sauce—its consistency is up to you, but many cooks make their sauces too thick; add 1 or 2 teaspoons water to thin it or simmer the sauce for a moment to reduce and thicken it. Whisk in the cold butter, keeping the pan and whisk moving until all the butter melts. (Don't let it sit without whisking or the butter will separate.) Season to taste with salt, pepper, and if necessary, a few more drops of vinegar.

Slice the breasts crosswise, arrange the slices on individual heated plates, and spoon the sauce over the breasts. Serve hot, with the orange wedges if desired.

VARIATION: You can substitute two Pekin duck breasts plus two braised duck legs (see page 36) or slow-roasted duck legs (see page 70). If you're using the braised duck legs, pull off the skin and discard it and pull the meat away from the bone. To reheat the duck meat, put it in a small saucepan—it's okay if it's a bit shredded—with ¼ cup of the braising liquid, cover the pan, and put it over low heat. You can also reheat it in the microwave.

For the sauce, reduce another 1¼ cup of the braising liquid in a small saucepan until it's lightly syrupy and measures about ½ cup. You can flavor the reduced braising liquid as described in the recipe above, using the juice of virtually any fruit. (Usually the juice is released as the fruit, say peaches, is lightly cooked, not by processing the fruit in a juicer.) The sauce may also be finished with about 4 tablespoons heavy cream or 2 tablespoons butter.

Cutting Perfect Orange Wedges

To cut an orange into membraneless, pithless wedges, slice both ends off the orange with a sharp paring knife, cutting deep enough that you can see the orange flesh. Set the orange on one end and carve off the peel, working from the top down and following the contours of the orange to leave as little flesh attached to the peel as possible.

When you've removed all the peel—and with it, the white pith—hold the orange in one hand over a bowl and slice along both sides of each of the thin membranes to separate each wedge from the others, coaxing the wedges into the bowl as you go. When all the wedges are in the bowl, squeeze the juice out of what's left of the orange over them. The wedges—now called "supremes"—are ready to use as a garniture for duck à l'orange.

Duck and Vegetables

Even the most elegant and elaborate duck dishes can be made in the same way as duck with peas. The only tricky part is cooking the vegetables so they're done at the same time as the duck. Here are a few ways to cook vegetables that can be combined with the duck sauce or served separately on the plate.

Pearl onions: For 6 servings, peel 1 pint of pearl onions and put them in a saucepan just large enough to hold them in a single layer. Add enough water or broth to come halfway up the sides of the onions and sprinkle them with salt, pepper, and a pinch of sugar. Add 1 tablespoon butter and put the pan, partially covered, over medium heat. Cook for about 15 minutes, until the onions are easily penetrated with a knife and all the surrounding liquid caramelizes—be careful not to let it burn—on the bottom of the pan. (If the liquid evaporates before the onions are done, add a few tablespoons more water or broth, leave off the lid, and turn up the heat.) Just before serving, add 1 tablespoon water or broth to the pan, reheat the onions, and serve them next to the sliced duck breast.

Spinach: For 6 servings, rinse the leaves from two 10-ounce bunches spinach and plunge them in a pot of well-salted boiling water for 30 seconds. Drain in a colander and rinse under cold water. Gently squeeze the spinach with your hands to extract excess water. Five minutes before you're ready to serve, boil ¼ cup heavy cream in a saucepan; season with salt and pepper. When the cream thickens—almost to the point where it's going to separate—add the spinach and stir for about 2 minutes to heat the spinach through. Place a small mound of spinach on each plate and arrange the duck breasts, whole or in slices, around or over the spinach.

Turnips: Look for baby turnips, which don't need to be peeled or shaped. Depending on their size, count on about 20 baby turnips for 4 servings. Cut off the long stringlike roots and all except ½ inch of the greens. Cook the turnips the same way as the pearl onions, except for 20 to 25 minutes. If you can only find large turnips, peel them and cut them into elongated rectangles as long as the turnip is high (about 1½ to 2 inches long and ½ inch thick on each side). Use a paring knife to round the edges, then cook in the same way as the baby turnips.

Score, season, and sauté the duck breasts according to the directions on page 14. Pour the fat out of the pan and deglaze the pan with about ¼ cup Madeira or port, whisk in ¼ cup homemade duck glaze or the equivalent (see page 9), and finish with 2 tablespoons cold butter. If you need to, reheat the turnips in the sauce before adding the butter, then spoon the turnips and sauce over the sliced duck breast and serve.

Duck with Peas

*M*uch like duck with fruit sauces, once you've cooked duck with vegetables, the possibilities for improvisation are limitless. Traditional recipes in which the duck is roasted whole call for surrounding the roasting duck with the vegetable in question, allowing enough time for the vegetable to cook. Duck with turnips, celery root, or carrots is made in more or less the same way. Because I cook duck in pieces instead of whole, I had to devise another system for cooking the vegetables. Easiest and most obvious was to simply cook the vegetable separately and either reheat it in the sauce or serve it on the side.

Peas are one of the few vegetables that are usually better frozen than fresh. Except for a couple of weeks in June, when local baby peas show up at the farmers' market, fresh peas are too big, too starchy, and not sweet enough. The trick to frozen peas is to disobey the directions on the package that say to cook them in boiling water. This is superfluous, since the peas have already been cooked at the factory—cooking them a second time will only rob them of flavor and texture. Simply reheat the thawed peas in butter or in the duck sauce.

MAKES 4 MAIN-COURSE SERVINGS

4 Pekin (Long Island) duck breasts or 2 mullard breasts (1½ to 2 pounds total),
  or 2 Pekin duck breasts plus 2 braised duck legs (see page 36)
Salt and pepper
1 cup concentrated duck broth, ¼ cup homemade duck glaze, 2 tablespoons commercial glaze
  (see pages 8 to 11), or, if using braised duck legs, 1½ cups of the braising liquid cooked down to ½ cup
½ cup Madeira or port
1½ pounds fresh baby peas, shelled, or one 10-ounce package frozen baby peas, thawed
1 tablespoon sherry vinegar or red wine vinegar, or more to taste
2 tablespoons cold unsalted butter

Use a sharp knife to score the skin side of the duck breasts in two directions, about 20 slashes per direction (see page 14 for more detailed instructions). Season the breasts on both sides with salt and pepper. If you're using the braised legs, pull away and discard the skin, and pull the meat off the bone in chunks. Reserve in the refrigerator.

If you're using the concentrated duck broth, reduce it in a small saucepan to ¼ cup glaze and reserve. Heat a

sauté pan over medium to high heat and sauté the duck breasts, skin side down, 8 to 10 minutes for the Pekin duck breasts and 12 to 18 minutes for the mullard. Turn the breasts over, adjust the heat to high, and cook for 1 minute for the Pekin duck and 2 minutes for the mullard. Pour the fat out of the pan and deglaze the pan with the Madeira.

While the duck is cooking, prepare the peas. If you're using fresh peas, bring 2 quarts water to a simmer in a saucepan with 2 tablespoons salt. Boil the peas for 1 minute and drain them in a strainer. Transfer the cooked fresh peas or the thawed frozen peas to the pan that you deglazed with the Madeira and put the pan over medium heat.

Use a whisk to add the concentrated broth, commercial glaze, or reduced braising liquid. If at this point the sauce seems too thick, thin it with a teaspoon or two of water; if it seems too thin, boil it to reduce it until it has a slightly syrupy consistency. Add the vinegar and simmer the sauce for about 30 seconds, then whisk in the butter—keep the pan and whisk moving until it all melts. Season to taste with salt, pepper, and if necessary, more vinegar.

Slice the breasts crosswise, arrange the slices on individual heated plates, and if you're using the duck legs, warm the meat and place a mound of it to the side of the breast meat. Spoon the sauce and peas over the duck and serve.

A Study in Contrasts

You can combine duck almost limitlessly with ingredients that provide contrasts in color, flavor, and texture. When thinking up a new dish, it helps to visualize how the foods will appear on the finished plate or occasionally a platter. In fact, I find that visually appealing combinations are often correspondingly satisfying to eat. When duck breast is served with baby peas, as in the recipe above, the contrast between green and brown is direct and dramatic. But keep in mind that some of the most dramatic dishes have only one color. The duck with foie gras that follows is a study in shades of brown—but nonetheless exciting. And don't forget about the color of the serving plate. You may want the color to contrast (as in the photo of duck with peas on page 22), or harmonize (like the dish with slow-roasted duck legs on page ii), or stick with a neutral white plate.

When imagining a finished dish, keep in mind how the flavors will interact. Perhaps you want the sauce to intensify the flavors of the duck, or maybe you'd prefer a direct contrast. Most French dishes are designed to concentrate and underline the intrinsic flavors of foods, while Thai dishes, for example, contrast the central element with the push and pull of sweet and sour, pungent and aromatic.

The duck with foie gras and artichokes on page 27, illustrates the importance of texture in a finished dish. The duck provides meaty and lightly chewy substance, the artichokes a subtle, nutlike resistance, and the foie gras an irresistibly silky, almost liquid mouth feel. I often include as many textures as possible without making the dish confusing to eat. If, for example, you decide to serve duck breast on a smooth mound of puréed potatoes flavored with garlic, you may want to include walnuts or pine nuts in the sauce to provide crunch. Or consider pairing the dish with braised root vegetables to add a soft, chewy texture somewhere between the nuts and the purée.

Duck with Foie Gras and Artichokes

$\mathcal{I}$t's not surprising that foie gras, the liver of specially fattened ducks and geese, is a delicious match for sautéed duck breasts. Foie gras is sold in several forms: the whole, raw, and enormous (about 1½ pounds) liver; the cooked and puréed liver called mousse; and the whole liver baked in a terrine mold, labeled "terrine of foie gras" with the words *bloc* or *entier* to distinguish it from the mousse. Most cooks who serve hot foie gras opt for cooking the whole livers. I prefer to cook slices of foie gras terrine, since much of the liver's moisture is cooked off in the terrine, making the foie gras denser and delightfully unctuous. But whole raw livers will also work for this recipe; you just have to be very careful not to overcook them.

Foie gras can be combined with duck in several ways. After sautéing the duck breasts, you can make a sauce in the same pan—much like the orange sauce on page 18, but without the orange—and the foie gras, puréed with an equal amount of butter, can be whisked into the sauce for flavor and texture. Or the foie gras can be cut into cubes—so it doesn't lose its texture—and combined with the sauce immediately before serving. My favorite method, however, is to place slices of cooked foie gras right on top of the whole sautéed duck breasts. Here I go a step further and set each sautéed breast on a cooked artichoke bottom. The interplay of textures and flavors is hard to beat.

MAKES 6 MAIN-COURSE SERVINGS

6 Pekin (Long Island) duck breasts (about 2½ pounds total)
Salt and pepper
6 large artichokes, trimmed, cooked, and chokes removed
   (see "Turning" and Cooking Artichokes, page 26)
1½ cups concentrated duck broth, 6 tablespoons homemade duck glaze,
   or 3 tablespoons commercial glaze (see pages 8 to 11)
6 slices terrine of foie gras (about 2 ounces each), or
   6 slices of raw liver (about 3 ounces each)
½ cup Madeira or port
1 tablespoon finely chopped parsley
3 tablespoons cold unsalted butter
2 teaspoons sherry vinegar or red wine vinegar, or more to taste

Use a sharp knife to score the skin side of the duck breasts in two directions, about 20 slashes per direction (see page 14 for more detailed instructions). Season the breasts on both sides with salt and pepper. Reserve in the refrigerator until about 15 minutes before you're ready to cook.

Cut each prepared artichoke into about six slices and reserve them on a heat-proof plate. Cover them with an inverted plate, or plastic wrap if you'll heat the artichokes in a microwave, or aluminum foil if you'll use an oven. If you're using concentrated duck broth, reduce it to about ½ cup glaze and reserve.

Sauté the duck breasts as described on page 14, reserving the fat in the pan. Reheat the artichoke slices in the microwave or oven. Heat the fat in the sauté pan over high heat until it barely begins to smoke, sauté the foie gras slices for about 30 seconds on each side, and reserve. Pour the fat out of the pan (if it hasn't burned, save it) and whisk in the Madeira and then the glaze. Adjust the sauce's consistency by boiling it to reduce it or adding water to thin it. Add the parsley, whisk in the butter, and add the vinegar and salt and pepper to taste.

Arrange the artichoke slices on heated serving plates, place a duck breast on top of each, and then add a slice of foie gras. Spoon the sauce over the top and serve.

"Turning" and Cooking Artichokes

Cut the stem off the artichoke where it joins the base. Trim the leaves off the sides of the artichoke by rotating the artichoke against a sharp paring knife, keeping the knife perpendicular to the base; continue in this way until you see white appear on the sides of the artichoke. Reposition the artichoke in your hand so you can trim off the green leaves attached to the bottom, and continue in this way until you see the pale green of the artichoke bottom. Trim off any remaining green leaves where they join the base, about a third of the way up from the bottom, exposing the base of the artichoke and the choke. Repeat with the rest of the artichokes. Don't try to remove the chokes yet—it's much easier after the artichokes are cooked.

Because baby artichokes don't have a large enough choke to choke on, you don't ever have to remove it, and you don't have to waste so much of the artichoke. To trim a baby artichoke, first cut off the stem and the top half of the leaves. Rotate the artichoke against a sharp paring knife, cutting the leaves away from the sides. When you see no more dark green on the sides, trim off any dark green that's still attached to the base.

Put the "turned" artichokes—full or baby size—in a nonaluminum pot, and add enough water to cover liberally and a few tablespoons lemon juice and olive oil to keep the artichokes from turning dark. Simmer until a knife slides into the bottom of an artichoke but still offers some resistance, about 20 minutes. Drain the artichokes. To remove the choke from large artichokes, hold the still-hot bottom in a kitchen towel and use a tablespoon to pull on the choke, starting on the outside perimeter and working toward the center. Don't actually cut into the bottom of the choke with the spoon—just pulling the choke is enough.

Duck with Teriyaki Glaze

*T*eriyaki is the easiest of all sauces to make. Traditional recipes call for soy sauce, sake, and a sweet Japanese cooking wine called mirin, but half the time I substitute white wine for the sake, and I use sugar when I've run out of mirin. Teriyaki sauce becomes a glaze when you reduce it in a sauté pan containing cooking duck breasts, or when you repeatedly brush the sauce on duck breasts cooking on the grill.

In this recipe, some of the teriyaki is used to glaze the duck and some is poured over the duck as a sauce. If you want to prevent the sauce from dissolving the glaze on the surface of the duck, prop each duck breast on a mound of greens, such as spinach or watercress, and spoon the sauce around the greens.

MAKES 4 MAIN-COURSE SERVINGS

4 Pekin (Long Island) duck breasts or 2 mullard breasts (1½ to 2 pounds total)
Pepper
⅔ cup dark soy sauce, preferably a Japanese brand
¼ cup rice wine vinegar
4 teaspoons sugar
1 teaspoon dark sesame oil, preferably a Japanese brand
⅔ cup sake or dry white wine
1 scallion, green top discarded, sliced thin

Score the duck breasts as described on page 14 and season them on both sides with pepper. Refrigerate them, covered, until an hour before you're ready to cook.

Heat a sauté pan over medium to high heat and sauté the duck breasts, skin side down, about 8 minutes for the Pekin duck breasts and 10 to 14 minutes for the mullard, then pour out the fat. (If it's not burned, you can reserve it for another use.) Combine the soy sauce, vinegar, sugar, sesame oil, and sake in a small saucepan and bring the mixture to a simmer. Pour half the mixture into the sauté pan with the duck breasts and boil it over high heat to create a glaze—move the duck breasts around in the sauce as it reduces—about 2 minutes. Turn the breasts over and continue cooking on the fleshy side, about 1 minute. If the glaze starts to get too thick—you don't want to burn it—add 1 tablespoon water to the hot pan. Add the scallions to the teriyaki sauce remaining in the saucepan and simmer for 1 minute more.

Slice the duck breasts crosswise and arrange the slices on heated serving plates. Spoon the sauce over the duck and serve. If the sauce has cooled off, reheat it.

LEFT: *Duck with Teriyaki Glaze, with braised baby bok choy.*

Duck with Chihuacle Negro Sauce, Raisins, and Almonds

$\mathcal{C}$hihuacle negro chiles are my favorite of all dried chiles. They look a little like black bell peppers and have an amazingly subtle and complex flavor. If you can't find them, substitute other dried chiles, such as guajillos, mulatos, or anchos, either alone or in combination. Or use fresh poblano chiles—first char their skins over the stove or on the grill, then peel, seed, and chop them.

The sauce I describe here is made with concentrated duck broth, which gives it a note of richness, but you can use chicken broth, even low-sodium versions out of a can. If you like, you can make this sauce without the raisins, dried apricots, or almonds—the chiles and cilantro are delicious without them. This recipe makes about ⅓ cup per serving and contains a lot of solid ingredients, which you should just spoon over the sautéed duck breasts. Serve with corn tortillas gently warmed in the oven or in a skillet. if you like, wrap the duck, its sauce, and the solid ingredients in a tortilla to be eaten like a soft taco.

MAKES 6 MAIN-COURSE SERVINGS

2 dried chihuacle negro chiles, 3 smaller dried chiles,
    or 2 fresh poblano chiles, charred and peeled
1 tablespoon unsalted butter
1 small red onion, peeled and chopped fine
4 cloves garlic, peeled and chopped fine
1½ cups brown duck broth (see page 8), chicken broth (see page 10), or water
½ cup heavy cream
6 Pekin (Long Island) duck breasts or 3 mullard breasts (1½ to 2 pounds total)
½ cup golden raisins
½ cup dried apricots, cut into ¼-inch cubes
½ cup slivered almonds
1 tablespoon red wine vinegar, or more to taste
2 tablespoons finely chopped cilantro
Salt

If you're using dried chiles, cut off the stems, cut the chiles in half lengthwise, and rinse out the seeds. Soak them in hot water until they're soft and pliable, about 30 minutes, then chop fine. If you're using poblano chiles, seed and finely chop them after peeling off their charred skins.

Melt the butter in a saucepan over low to medium heat, add the onion and garlic, and cook until they're soft but not brown, about 15 minutes. Add the chiles, broth, and cream, and simmer the sauce gently for 15 minutes—it should remain thin and brothlike.

Transfer the sauce to a blender and purée for about 1 minute, starting with short pulses and holding the lid on firmly with a towel so the mixture doesn't shoot out. Use a small ladle to work the sauce through a fine-mesh strainer and into the rinsed-out saucepan.

Score, season, and sauté the duck breasts according to the directions on page 14. Reheat the sauce over low heat, stir in the raisins, apricots, almonds, vinegar, and cilantro, and bring to a gentle simmer. Season to taste with salt. Slice the breasts crosswise, arrange the slices on heated soup plates, spoon the sauce over them, and serve.

CHILE SAUCES FOR SAUTÉED DUCK BREASTS

You can get amazingly interesting and complex flavors out of chiles, especially dried ones. Make a simple sauce by soaking dried chiles in hot water—first cut them in half lengthwise and rinse out the seeds—and then puréeing the softened chiles in a blender with hot heavy cream and duck broth, or just the cream. I sometimes stir raisins into the sauce after puréeing for the welcome note of sweetness they provide, and I may also add slivered almonds for crunch. Chopped cilantro almost always works well with dried chiles. If you really want to get carried away, try making two or three dried chile sauces for subtle variations in flavor and color, then juxtapose them on the plate over or around the duck breast. Pomegranate seeds look great sprinkled over the sliced duck.

Unless you live in New Mexico, some of the more exotic chiles can be hard to find. It's worthwhile to order an assortment of them by mail to have on hand for quick sauces. See Sources, page 154, for two good suppliers.

Duck Breasts or Duck Legs with Pink Lentil Sauce

*F*rench cooks have long served lentil puree with game while Indian cooks have used lentils to make their almost universal dish, dhal. I've combined the two concepts to come up with a sauce for duck that's lightly flavored with cumin and ghee. The French use whole butter, but because ghee (called *beurre noisette,* or "hazelnut butter," by the French) has a more pronounced flavor of butter, you can use relatively little and still taste it. You can make this sauce as light or as rich as you like by adding varying amounts of ghee. Ideally the lentils should be cooked in broth, but even when they're made with water, this sauce is savory and satisfying. Here I call for pink or red lentils, but yellow and brown lentils will also work; their texture, once cooked, will be just slightly less fine.

MAKES 4 MAIN-COURSE SERVINGS

Four 6- to 8-ounce Pekin (Long Island) duck breasts, 4 slow-roasted duck legs
  (see page 70), or 4 braised duck legs (see page 36)
Salt and pepper
7 to 9 tablespoons unsalted butter
1 small onion, peeled and chopped
1 clove garlic, peeled and chopped
½ cup pink, red, yellow, or brown lentils, rinsed and drained in a fine-mesh strainer
2½ cups brown duck broth (see page 8), braising liquid from the duck legs
  (see page 36), chicken broth (see page 10), or water
¼ cup heavy cream
1 teaspoon ground cumin
2 teaspoons ground coriander
2 tablespoons chopped cilantro
1 teaspoon fresh lemon juice, or more to taste

Score the breasts as described on page 14 and season them with salt and pepper. Reserve in the refrigerator until needed.

Melt 1 tablespoon of the butter in a saucepan over low to medium heat, add the onion and garlic, and cook for about 10 minutes, until softened. Add the lentils and broth or water, partially cover the saucepan, and simmer gently until the lentils are completely soft, about 40 minutes. Stir in the cream and simmer for 1 minute more.

While the lentils are cooking, heat the remaining 6 to 8 tablespoons butter, as desired, over medium heat in a heavy-bottomed sauté pan. When the milk solids in the butter just begin to brown, after about 4 minutes, plunge the bottom of the pan into a bowl of cold water to stop the cooking and keep the milk solids from burning. Strain the ghee through a fine-mesh strainer or a piece of cheesecloth into a small saucepan. Don't fret if some of the caramelized milk solids get through the strainer.

Heat the ghee with the cumin and coriander over low heat until you smell their fragrance, about 1 minute. Stir the seasoned ghee into the lentil mixture, then work the lentils through a food mill or through a fine-mesh strainer into a small saucepan, using the back of a ladle. If the sauce is too thick—it should have the consistency of a cream soup—strain it again through a fine-mesh strainer, and if necessary, add more broth or water. Stir in the cilantro and lemon juice, and season to taste with salt and pepper.

If you're using duck breasts, sauté them as described on page 14. Ladle the sauce into heated soup plates and arrange the whole duck breasts on top of the sauce. (The duck isn't sliced or the slices would end up submerged in the sauce.) If you're using duck legs, separate the thighs from the drumsticks and reheat them in the sauce before arranging in heated soup plates. Serve with plenty of rice.

Braising

BRAISING AND STEWING are essentially the same thing—cooking in a small amount of liquid—except that stewing implies that the pieces of meat (or fish) are cut into relatively small pieces. I suppose that pot roast is the best known of all American braised dishes.

Duck legs are particularly well suited to braising and stewing because they are tough and need long cooking to soften them up. Yet compared to some stews, duck stew is rather quick to make, requiring about an hour and a half of braising. The braising liquid can be water, broth, wine, cider, beer—or virtually any flavorful liquid you can think of—and it can double as the sauce for the legs and also for sautéed breasts. Sometimes after braising duck legs and sautéing duck breasts, I use the braising liquid from the legs as the basis of a sauce for both.

Braised Duck Legs

MAKES 12 MAIN-COURSE SERVINGS

12 duck legs, including both thighs and drumsticks
Salt and pepper
4 to 6 tablespoons rendered duck fat (see page 15),
  unsalted butter, or vegetable oil
1 large carrot, peeled and chopped fine
½ stalk celery, chopped fine
1 large onion, peeled and chopped fine
4 cloves garlic, crushed, peeled, and chopped coarse
2 cups red or white wine
2 cups brown duck broth (see page 8), chicken broth (see pages 10), or water
1 bouquet garni (3 sprigs thyme, 3 sprigs parsley, and 1 imported bay leaf,
  tied together with kitchen twine)

PREVIOUS PAGE: *Duck Legs Braised with Indian Spices (recipe on page 38).*

Cut the drumsticks away from the thighs by slicing diagonally where the drumstick joins the thigh. Don't get frustrated; it takes some trial and error to find where the two meet. Season with salt and pepper. Heat 4 tablespoons of the duck fat in a heavy-bottomed pot over medium to high heat, add the duck legs, and brown them for about 8 minutes on each side. If you can't fit them in the pot in a single layer, brown them in batches. If at any point the fat in the pot smells burned, pour it out and replace it with 2 tablespoons new fat. When the legs are browned, remove them and reserve them on a platter.

Add the carrot, celery, onion, and garlic to the pot and stir them in the fat—use new fat if the fat is burned—over medium heat for about 10 minutes, until they just begin to brown. Pour in the wine and broth and nestle in the bouquet garni. Put the duck legs, skin side up, back in the pot, along with any juices that have run out onto the platter. Bring to a simmer over high heat, then lower the heat to maintain a gentle simmer. Don't worry if all the legs aren't submerged in the cooking liquid. Cover the top of the pot with a sheet of aluminum foil and press the foil down on the center, so the legs not covered with broth are basted on the inside of the pot.

Cover the pot with the lid and let the legs stew for 1 hour over low heat. Check them after 10 minutes to make sure they're at a low simmer—a bubble should rise gently to the surface every couple of seconds—and adjust the heat accordingly. After 30 minutes, rearrange the legs in the pot so those that were sticking out above the liquid are now submerged. If you're using the braised duck legs in another recipe and skipping the glazing stage below, simmer the legs for 1½ hours instead of just an hour.

Use a pair of tongs to transfer the legs to a platter. Strain the braising liquid through a fine-mesh sieve into a saucepan, pressing down with the back of a ladle on the aromatic vegetables and bouquet garni in the strainer to extract as much of the liquid as you can. Discard the vegetables and the bouquet garni. Set the saucepan over low to medium heat, a bit off-center on the burner so the braising liquid boils up on one side only. Use a small ladle or spoon to skim off any fat or froth that rises to the surface on the opposite side. Continue reducing and skimming for about 30 minutes, until the liquid has reduced to about 2 cups and you've skimmed off most of the fat.

Transfer the duck legs, skin side up, to a clean oven-proof pot or pan—ideally one just large enough to hold the legs in a single layer—and pour the reduced braising liquid over them. Set the oven on 400°F—you don't need to preheat—and slide in the duck legs, uncovered. Repeatedly baste the duck legs for 20 to 30 minutes, until they're covered with a shiny glaze. Season to taste with salt and pepper.

Serve each guest a braised drumstick and a thigh over a bed of creamed spinach, sorrel, or as in the recipe on page 41, red cabbage.

Duck Legs Braised with Indian Spices

They don't seem to cook a lot of duck in India—recipes are scarce—but the braising techniques used for lamb, which is served a lot, work in the same way for duck. You just have to be careful to eliminate most of the fat that the duck renders as it cooks. You can make this dish with both duck breasts and legs, or you can serve just legs and use the breasts for another recipe. This recipe makes a lot of sauce, so be sure to serve it with plenty of rice, preferably fragrant white basmati rice.

An ingredient that makes Indian food—and this dish—taste so good is the use of ghee. Ghee is clarified butter, but butter that's been clarified so the milk solids caramelize, giving it a characteristic butterscotch quality that in turn imparts a suave complexity to sauces and stews. And then there's the garam masala, a traditional north Indian spice mixture that I urge you to prepare (see recipe, opposite). Store-bought curry powder will seem drab after you taste this blend's subtle layers of flavor, and since you can store it in the freezer for up to a year, there's no excuse not to make a generous batch to have at the ready.

MAKES 6 MAIN-COURSE SERVINGS

6 duck legs, including both thighs and drumsticks
Salt and pepper
3 tablespoons vegetable oil
1 stick (8 tablespoons) unsalted butter
2 medium onions, peeled and chopped fine
2 tablespoons grated fresh ginger
2 garlic cloves, peeled and chopped fine
1 tablespoon Garam Masala Spice Mixture (see page 39)
    or good-quality curry powder
2 cups brown duck broth (see page 8), chicken broth
    (see page 10), or water
1 cup heavy cream
1 cup plain yogurt

Cut the drumsticks away from the thighs (see page 37) and season both thighs and drumsticks with salt and pepper. Heat the vegetable oil in a heavy-bottomed pot over medium to high heat, then brown the thighs and drumsticks for about 8 minutes on each side. Take the duck parts out of the pot and reserve.

Pour the cooked fat out of the pot—don't bother saving it, since it will most likely be a little burned—and replace it with 2 tablespoons of the butter. Put the pot over medium heat, add the onions, and stir every few minutes until they soften and turn translucent, about 20 minutes. Stir in the ginger, garlic, and spice mixture and cook for about 1 minute, until you smell their fragrance. Nestle in the duck pieces and pour the broth or water over all. Bring to a simmer, cover, and cook gently, so a bubble rises up every second or so. Braise in this way for 1½ hours.

While the duck is cooking, heat the remaining 6 tablespoons butter in a heavy-bottomed saucepan over medium heat until the specks of milk solids turn pale brown, about 4 minutes, and the butter—now ghee—is clear and fragrant. Plunge the bottom of the pan into a bowl of cold water to stop the cooking, then strain the ghee through a fine-mesh strainer or cheesecloth and reserve.

Use tongs to gently transfer the duck pieces to a bowl, and pour the braising liquid into a glass pitcher. Skim off any fat and scum with a ladle and return the braising liquid to the pot. Boil it down until there's just enough liquid to coat the onions, then stir in the heavy cream and yogurt. Add the duck legs, lower the heat, and simmer gently, uncovered, for 15 minutes. Then stir in the ghee in a thin, steady stream. (Don't add it too quickly or it won't emulsify with the rest of the sauce.) Season to taste with salt and pepper. Serve in heated soup plates to catch the sauce. Pass plenty of basmati rice at the table.

Garam Masala Spice Mixture

The closest most of us get to authentic Indian cooking is our use of a little curry powder. This is a pity, since adding curry powder to every Indian dish is roughly analogous to using the same dried herb mix for any dish that's French. The greatness of Indian cooking is its subtle use of various spice mixtures.

I got the idea for this recipe from Julie Sahni's wonderful primer, Classic Indian Cooking. In her book, Sahni describes two spice mixtures that are almost universal in northern Indian cooking. The first, and the one I use here, is Moghul garam masala, a mixture of cardamom (preferably the harder-to-find black cardamom), cinnamon, cloves, black pepper, and nutmeg. Regular garam masala adds to this large quantities of coriander and cumin. The spice mixture used in this recipe is a variation of Mughal garam masala that contains cumin. You can grind your own spices using a blender, or use preground spices to make your own garam masala.

To make ½ cup, combine 2 tablespoons ground cardamom (preferably the black variety), 1 tablespoon ground cinnamon, 2 teaspoons ground cloves, 1 tablespoon freshly ground black pepper, 1 teaspoon ground nutmeg, and 2 tablespoons ground cumin and mix well. I make extras of my favorite spice mixtures and keep them in an airtight container in the freezer, where they hold their flavor for up to 1 year. Indian cooks traditionally roast their spices just before they use them; I cook the spice mixture in butter for an effect very similar to pre-roasting.

Braised or Slow-Roasted Duck Legs
with Red Cabbage and Juniper Berries

*U*se either braised or roasted duck legs for this dish. If you're making the recipe with roasted duck legs, use broth or water instead of the braising liquid.

MAKES 6 MAIN-COURSE SERVINGS

6 braised duck legs (see page 36) and 2 cups of the braising liquid
  before it's reduced, or 6 slow-roasted duck legs (see page 70) and 3 cups
  brown duck broth (see page 8) or chicken broth (see page 10)
1 medium red cabbage
3 tart baking apples
Juice of 1 lemon (about 3 tablespoons)
2 tablespoons rendered duck fat (see page 15) or unsalted butter
1 large red onion, peeled and sliced thin
10 juniper berries, crushed under a saucepan
3 tablespoons balsamic vinegar, or more to taste
Salt and pepper

If you're using the braised duck legs, follow the recipe up to the point where you've strained and degreased the braising liquid but haven't yeat reduced it, and reserve both.

Cut the stem off the cabbage where it joins at the base, and quarter the cabbage vertically. Cut out and discard the strip of white core that runs along each of the four wedges, then slice the wedges, crosswise, as thin as you can.

Peel the apples and cut them into ½-inch cubes. Toss them with the lemon juice and reserve. (Don't soak them in water and lemon juice as many recipes recommend because the water will leach out their sugar and flavor.)

Melt the duck fat over medium heat in a heavy-bottomed ovenproof pan just large enough to hold the duck legs in a single layer. Add the onion and stir it every few minutes for about 20 minutes.

Meanwhile, preheat the oven to 350°F. Add the cabbage and juniper berries to the pan and stir every few minutes until the cabbage wilts and shrinks, about 20 minutes more. Stir in the apple cubes and nestle the duck legs, skin side up, in the cabbage.

Pour the braising liquid or broth into the pan and bake, partially covered, for 30 minutes. Add the vinegar to taste and season with salt and pepper. Place a mound of cabbage on each heated soup plate with a duck leg—a drumstick and thigh if you've separated them—on top. Ladle the cooking liquid over all and serve.

Duck Leg Stew with Wild Mushrooms

*T*his recipe offers another way to serve the duck legs that you've stockpiled in the freezer after you've grilled or sautéed the breasts. The braising liquid can be used in a sauce for the duck legs (see the variation, opposite), or for the legs and breasts served together on the same plate. While serving this dish topped with sautéed wild mushrooms takes it to new heights of elegance, regular cultivated mushrooms or cremini mushrooms, quartered vertically, will provide an excellent flavor and contrasting texture.

MAKES 6 GENEROUS OR 12 LIGHT MAIN-COURSE SERVINGS

12 duck legs, including both thighs and drumsticks
2 cloves garlic, peeled and chopped
2 medium onions, peeled and chopped coarse
1 carrot, peeled and sliced
2 cups red wine
1 bouquet garni (5 sprigs fresh thyme or ½ teaspoon dried,
* 1 imported bay leaf, and 1 bunch parsley or parsley stems,*
* tied together with kitchen twine or wrapped in cheesecloth)*
Salt and pepper
7 tablespoons unsalted butter
2 cups brown duck broth (see page 8) or chicken broth (see page 10)
1½ pounds assorted wild or cultivated mushrooms, such as chanterelles,
* morels, porcini, and hedgehogs, rinsed and patted dry*
1 tablespoon finely chopped parsley

Put the duck legs in a large nonreactive bowl and add the garlic, onions, carrot, red wine, and bouquet garni. Let the duck marinate overnight in the refrigerator.

Strain the duck legs and reserve the liquid and the vegetables separately. Reserve the bouquet garni, too. Pat the legs dry—wipe off any clinging vegetables that would burn—and season them on both sides with salt and pepper.

In one or two skillets over medium heat, melt 3 tablespoons of the butter and brown the legs on both sides, 6 to 8 minutes on each side. Transfer the legs to a plat-ter, pour the cooked butter out of the skillet, and add 2 more tablespoons of the butter and the vegetables from the marinade. Stir the vegetables over medium heat until they smell fragrant and the onions turn translucent, about 12 minutes. Put the legs back in the skillet (at this point the legs don't have to stay in a single layer), pour the marinade liquid and the broth or water over all, and nestle in the reserved bouquet garni. Bring to a gentle simmer, cover the skillet, and cook—over low heat or in a 325°F oven—for 2 hours. After 1 hour of cooking, gently shift the legs that were in the bottom of the skillet to the top.

Gently remove the duck legs from the skillet with a skimmer or slotted spoon and transfer them to a plate. Cover the legs with aluminum foil to keep them from darkening. Strain the braising liquid into a saucepan and bring to a gentle simmer, discarding the vegetables. Put the pan slightly off-center on the heat source so it only bubbles up on one side, and use a spoon or small ladle to scoop off any fat or scum that floats to the surface on the other side. Wash the skillet used to braise the legs and put the legs back in. When the braising liquid has cooked down to half, pour it over the duck legs, put on the lid, and reheat the legs over low heat for 30 minutes. Season to taste with salt and pepper.

Shortly before you're ready to serve, sauté the wild mushrooms in the remaining 2 tablespoons butter over high heat for about 5 minutes. Season with salt and pepper and reserve.

Serve each person one or two duck legs in a heated soup plate, with the braising liquid spooned over and around and the mushrooms and parsley on top.

VARIATION: You can convert the finished braising liquid from the duck legs into a sauce in one of two ways. In the first method, simmer down the braising liquid until it's reduced to 1 cup. Use the back of a fork to work 1 tablespoon flour with 1 tablespoon softened unsalted butter to create a smooth paste—the French call this mixture a *beurre manié,* or "kneaded butter"—and whisk the paste into the simmering braising liquid. Simmer and whisk the sauce until it thickens, about 30 seconds. For an even more intensely flavored sauce, reduce the braising liquid to ½ cup over medium heat—with the pan moved to one side to maintain a gentle simmer and make it easy to skim off fat and froth—then whisk in 4 tablespoons cold unsalted butter.

Reducing and Degreasing

Even though the word "reduce" is almost ubiquitous in kitchens and cookbooks, I run into people who don't know that it's just a fancy way of saying "boil down." Usually we reduce broths or stewing liquids to concentrate them and to accentuate flavor and sometimes texture. But there's another purpose behind reducing broths—getting rid of their fat by degreasing.

When reducing broth, it should never be allowed to boil, because fat and particles of protein, which float to the top, get churned back into the broth if it boils, making the sauce or stewing liquid greasy and hard to digest. Instead, set the saucepan or pot off-center over the flame or heat source so that the liquid simmers on just one side. This pushes fat and scum (protein) to the other side, making it easier to skim it off with a ladle or kitchen spoon. One of the easiest ways to degrease a pot of broth is to refrigerate it overnight and then just use a spoon to lift off the congealed fat that forms on top.

Cassoulet with Braised Duck Legs

*T*his is an easy and less rich version of cassoulet that substitutes braised duck legs for confit duck legs. It still has plenty of flavor because you cook the beans in the braising liquid from the duck legs. Feel free to make half as much as called for here.

MAKES 12 MAIN-COURSE SERVINGS

2 pounds (4½ cups) dried white beans,
*   such as borlotti, cannellini, or great Northern*
1 pig's foot, halved lengthwise
*   (ask your butcher to do this; optional)*
12 duck legs, including both thighs and drumsticks
Salt and pepper
3 tablespoons rendered duck fat (see page 15) or vegetable oil
1 bouquet garni (3 sprigs thyme or 2 teaspoons dried thyme,
*   3 sprigs parsley, and 1 imported bay leaf, tied together*
*   with kitchen twine or wrapped in cheesecloth)*
2 medium onions, peeled
2 whole cloves, stuck into one of the onions
1 large carrot, peeled and cut into 4 cylinders
4 cloves garlic, crushed and peeled, plus 1 clove garlic,
*   peeled and left whole*
2 quarts brown duck broth (see page 8), chicken broth (see page 10),
*   or water, or more as needed*
4 cups fresh coarse bread crumbs, made from 1 loaf
*   dense-crumb white bread*
1 garlic or duck sausage (see page 107), raw or precooked,
*   12 inches long and 2 inches thick*

Rinse the beans and put them in a bowl with enough water to cover by at least 8 inches—that way, as the beans expand, they'll still be covered. Let soak for 12 hours, then drain.

If using, put the pig's foot halves in a pot, cover with cold water, and bring to a boil over high heat. Boil for 5 minutes, drain in a colander, and rinse thoroughly under cold running water.

Season the duck legs on both sides with salt and pepper, then put them in a heavy-bottomed pot with the duck fat and brown them over medium to high heat, about 10 minutes on each side. Take the legs out of the pot with tongs and pour out the burnt fat. Put the legs back in the pot and add the blanched pig's foot, bouquet garni, onions (including the one with cloves), carrot, and crushed garlic. Pour over enough of the broth or water to cover by 3 inches and bring to a gentle simmer. Cook for about 15 minutes, skimming off any froth or fat that floats to the top. Cover the pot, turn the heat down to low, and cook for 1 hour.

Sprinkle with ½ teaspoon salt or more to taste, and add the drained beans and enough broth or water to cover by an inch. Cover the pot again, return to a simmer, and cook for 45 minutes more. Gently stir the beans with a wooden spoon once or twice, scraping against the bottom of the pot to make sure they're not sticking and scalding. If the beans start to run dry, add more broth or water.

Remove the pig's foot, onion, carrots, and bouquet garni with a pair of tongs, discarding the vegetables and bouquet garni. Cut any of the gelatinous meat covering the pig's foot into ½-inch dice and stir it into the beans. Taste the beans for salt—they'll be mealy, but don't worry—and season as needed.

Preheat the oven to 350°F. Rub the inside of a large baking dish, large roasting pan, or one or more gratin dishes with the whole peeled garlic clove. With a slotted spoon, transfer half the beans and the diced foot gel atin into the prepared dish or pan, leaving the liquid behind in the pot. Arrange the duck legs on top of the bean mixture, then add the rest of the bean mixture, again leaving the liquid behind in the pot. Finally, bring the bean-cooking liquid to a simmer and ladle over enough of it to come three quarters of the way up the sides of the beans, reserving any liquid you haven't used.

Spread the top of the cassoulet with about a third of the bread crumbs and slide it into the oven. When the cassoulet is bubbling and the bread crumbs have formed a crust, about 30 minutes, gently push the crust down into the beans with a large spoon. Sprinkle the top of the beans again with half of the remaining bread crumbs. If at any point the cassoulet seems dry and stiff, add 1 cup of the reserved bean-cooking liquid (or water if you run out of liquid). Bake for 1 hour more, until a second crust has formed, then push the crust into the beans as before. Nestle in the sausage—if it's thick, you can cut it into 1-inch lengths—pushing some of the beans to the side and folding them over the sausage. Sprinkle with the rest of the bread crumbs and bake until a final crust has formed, about 1 hour more; serve hot.

Duck Leg Tagine

*T*agines are a kind of flavorful Moroccan stew often enhanced with dried fruits and almonds. To make a basic tagine, braise duck legs in broth or water, and then flavor the braising liquid with saffron, ginger, and ground coriander. You can also mimic the same effect by using slow-roasted duck legs and substituting duck or chicken broth for the braising liquid. Add slivered almonds, raisins, dried apricots, black olives, and if you have them, preserved lemons (see page 48). You can make your own variations by spooning over cooked vegetables such as carrots, artichokes, or zucchini. Last, but perhaps most important, serve your tagines—duck and otherwise—with harissa, an aromatic chile paste. I serve duck tagine with couscous.

MAKES 6 MAIN-COURSE SERVINGS

6 braised duck legs, braised for 1½ hours instead of 1 hour (see page 36),
    or 6 slow-roasted duck legs (see page 70), skin on or off
1 cup braising liquid from the duck legs, brown duck broth (see page 8),
    or chicken broth (see page 10)
½ cup dried apricots, chopped coarse
½ cup raisins, preferably golden
1 teaspoon saffron threads, soaked for 30 minutes
    in 1 tablespoon water
1 tablespoon grated fresh ginger
1 teaspoon ground turmeric
1 teaspoon ground cinnamon
¼ teaspoon ground cloves
½ cup slivered almonds, toasted for 15 minutes
    in a 350°F oven, until fragrant and pale brown
½ cup medium black, red, or green olives,
    or a combination, pitted and halved
1 wedge preserved lemon (see page 48),
    cut into ⅛-inch dice (optional)
Salt
1 recipe harissa (see page 49)

RIGHT: *Duck tagine served with couscous, harissa, and preserved lemons.*

In a large pot, gently reheat the duck legs in the braising liquid or broth. Stir in the apricots, raisins, saffron with its soaking liquid, ginger, turmeric, cinnamon, and cloves and bring the stew to a simmer, cooking for about 30 minutes.

Just before you're ready to serve, sprinkle in the toasted almonds, olives, and preserved lemon if using, and season to taste with salt. Put the duck legs—a drumstick and a thigh if you've separated them—in heated soup plates and spoon the sauce over them. Serve the harissa at the table for guests to dollop on the duck.

Preserved Lemons

When preserved for several weeks (or months) in salt, lemons develop an intense flavor that makes them a useful flavoring in combination with dried fruits, nuts, and spices. Preserved lemons take 3 weeks to make, but once you have them, they keep forever. I've stored mine in the back of the refrigerator for 2 years.

MAKES 1 QUART

9 lemons, preferably the more aromatic Meyer lemons
5 tablespoons coarse salt

Scrub the lemons and cut off the brown end where the stem once was. Cut 5 of the lemons into 4 wedges each and stack them in a 1-quart mason jar, sprinkling them, as you go, with the salt. Press them down firmly into the jar, so that when you add the lemon juice, they'll be mostly covered. Squeeze the remaining 4 lemons and pour the juice into the jar. Screw on the top, turn the jar over a couple of times to dissolve the salt, and let it sit in the refrigerator for 2 days. Turn the jar over and let it sit for 3 days more. Continue in this way, turning the jar over every 2 days, for 2 more weeks. The preserved lemons are now ready to use. Refrigerate until needed.

Harissa

*H*arissa is an irresistible paste-like sauce made with dried chiles—it's fun to experiment with different kinds—plus cumin, coriander, and sometimes caraway. The stuff is so addictive, and makes such a perfect counterpoint to the dried fruits in a tagine, you'll find yourself smearing it over the duck in rather shocking amounts.

MAKES ABOUT 1 CUP

10 dried chiles, such as anchos, guajillos, mulatos, or chihuacle negros
1 large clove garlic, peeled, chopped fine, and crushed to a paste
  with the side of a chefs' knife
1 teaspoon ground coriander
1 teaspoon gound cumin
½ cup water
1 tablespoon fresh lemon juice, or more to taste

Cut the stems off the chiles, slice them in half lengthwise, and rinse out the seeds. Soak for 1 hour in hot water, then discard the bitter water. In a blender, combine the chiles with the garlic, ground coriander, and ground cumin. Add the ½ cup water and purée until smooth. If the mixture is too stiff to blend, add a little more water—the harissa should have the consistency of a thick sauce. Stir in the lemon juice, adding more to taste, if necessary. Store covered in the refrigerator. I've kept harissa for weeks with no problems, but to be safe, count on using it within 1 week.

Duck Legs with Mole Sauce

For those of us who think mole sauce tastes mostly of chocolate, it comes as a pleasant surprise to discover that most of its flavor comes from dried chiles. Dried chiles have an amazing array of complex flavors that blend easily into a harmonious sauce. Chocolate, if used at all, is incorporated in such small quantities that it's almost impossible to identify.

Mole is a perfect way to use any duck legs you've been accumulating in the freezer, from those ducks whose breasts you've already cooked. Writers about Mexican food—Rick Bayless and Diana Kennedy are my two favorites—give very specific recipes for lots of different moles, but I think it's more fun to improvise, using recipes as points of reference. Unlike most European cooks, who start their stews by cooking aromatic vegetables in a little oil, Mexican cooks prefer to toast the vegetables in a hot skillet, either on the stove or in the oven, a trick that gives the vegetables a complexity that complements the flavor of the chiles. Nuts and seeds are used to thicken the sauce, and are sometimes left whole to provide crunch.

This duck mole is relatively simple, requiring fewer steps and fewer ingredients than traditional versions, but nonetheless it's a delicious dish. If you can't find all the chiles listed here, just use more of the others. For mail-order sources, see page 154.

MAKES 8 MAIN-COURSE SERVINGS

1 large white or yellow onion, peeled and quartered

1 medium carrot, peeled and cut into 3-inch cylinders

6 cloves garlic, peeled

8 duck legs, including both thighs and drumsticks

Salt and pepper

3 tablespoons rendered duck fat (see page 15) or olive oil

2 cups brown duck broth (see page 8), chicken broth (see page 10),
   or water, or more as needed

2 pounds ripe tomatoes, chopped (don't bother peeling and seeding)

1 dried chipotle (smoked jalapeño) chile

3 dried ancho or guajillo chiles

3 dried mulato chiles

3 dried chihuacle chiles, preferably chihuacle negros

¼ cup all-natural peanut butter or cashew butter (nuts and salt
   should be the only ingredients; see Nut Butters, page 51)

4 tablespoons lime juice (about 2 limes' worth), or more to taste

½ cup slivered almonds, toasted for 15 minutes in a 350°F oven,
   until fragrant and pale brown

Sour cream (optional)

In a heavy-bottomed, ovenproof saucepan, toss together the onion, carrot, and garlic. Set the oven on 400°F—there's no need to preheat. Roast the vegetables, stirring every 10 minutes, until they are brown around the edges and smell toasty, about 30 minutes. Break apart the onion quarters and allow the slices to blacken on the edges, another 10 minutes.

While the vegetables are roasting, season the duck legs on both sides with salt and pepper, then put them, along with the duck fat, in a heavy-bottomed pot and brown them over medium to high heat, about 10 minutes on each side. Using tongs, transfer the duck legs to a plate and discard the cooked fat left in the pot. Put the legs back in the pot, pour the broth or water over them, and add the tomatoes. Bring to a gentle simmer—with a bubble rising every second or two—and cover the pot.

When the vegetables are ready, put them in the pot with the duck. If there's not enough liquid in the pot to come halfway up the bottom layer of legs, add more broth or water. After the duck legs have cooked for 30 minutes, rearrange them, submerging any that were above the liquid. Simmer gently for 1 to 1½ hours in all, until a skewer slides easily in and out of a leg.

While the duck is simmering, wipe the chiles with a damp towel and put them in a heavy iron skillet over high heat. Turn the chiles over and around with a pair of tongs—don't let them burn—and when they smell fragrant, after 1 or 2 minutes, take them out of the skillet and let them cool. Cut off the stems, halve each chile lengthwise, and brush out the seeds. Put the chiles in a bowl, cover them with hot tap water, and let them soak for 30 minutes to an hour, then drain them. Don't save the soaking water, which is often bitter.

When the duck legs are done, transfer them to a plate and wipe off any tomato peels or vegetables left clinging to them. Strain the braising liquid into a clean saucepan, pressing down on the vegetables with a ladle to extract all their juices and discarding what doesn't go through. Place the pot with the braising liquid off-center over the flame so it simmers only on one side and pushes the fat floating on top to the opposite side, making it easier to skim. Every 5 minutes, skim off the fat and any froth with a small ladle. Reduce to about 2 cups.

Put the chiles, peanut butter, and duck braising liquid in a blender and start puréeing in short pulses on the lowest speed while holding the top firmly with a towel. (Puréeing hot liquids too suddenly can cause them to shoot out the top of the blender.) Purée for 2 minutes, until smooth. If the sauce is too thick—it should be soupy, not pasty—thin it with a little broth or water. Add the lime juice to the sauce and season to taste with salt. Reheat the duck legs in the mole sauce and transfer to heated soup plates. Sprinkle the almonds on top, and serve with plenty of rice, passing the sour cream.

Nut Butters

Peanut butter and other nut butters are used in Brazilian, Thai, and Mexican cooking to thicken and flavor sauces. They are marvelous with the coconut milk common in Thai and Brazilian cooking and with the spices and chiles found in Mexican cooking. When buying peanut butter or other nut butters, make sure that the only ingredients are the nuts in question and perhaps some salt. Many brands of peanut butter contain hydrogenated fats and emulsifiers to make the peanut butter unnaturally smooth.

You can make your own nut butters by simply grinding nuts in a food processor; add a little bit of water or appropriate oil (peanut oil for peanut butter) to keep the mixture turning around. If you want to make a nut butter to thicken a sauce, just put the nuts in question in the bowl of a food processor, purée them until smooth, and then slowly add the liquid for your sauce.

Duck Legs with Thai Green Curry

*U*nlike the familiar powdered curry, Thai curry is a paste made by pounding fresh aromatic ingredients and herbs with a mortar and pestle. Although a food processor does a halfway decent job, unless you're willing to sit for hours in front of a giant mortar (I'm not), you'll never get a perfectly smooth paste. My own solution involves deconstructing the curry paste into its various attractive components: cilantro, lemongrass, kaffir lime leaves, chiles, and galangal—a rhizome that looks something like ginger but has a distinct and completely different pinelike aroma and flavor. Because Thai curry dishes are unthickened and on the runny side, serve them in wide soup plates and pass plenty of rice.

MAKES 6 MAIN-COURSE SERVINGS

12 duck legs
Salt and pepper
3 tablespoons peanut oil
2 medium onions, chopped fine
3 cups brown duck broth or chicken broth (see pages 8 or 10)
2 stalks lemongrass
Four ½-inch-thick slices galangal (available at Asian groceries)
4 fresh or frozen kaffir lime leaves (available at Asian groceries),
    or the zest of 1 lime
Juice of 4 limes (about ½ cup)
3 cloves garlic, peeled, chopped fine, and crushed to a paste with
    the side of a chefs' knife
3 Thai chiles or 6 jalapeño chiles, stemmed, seeded, and chopped fine
One 14-ounce can unsweetened coconut milk
1 bunch cilantro, leaves only, chopped coarse
¼ cup Thai fish sauce, or more to taste

Season the duck legs with salt and pepper, and brown them in a heavy-bottomed pot in 2 tablespoons of the peanut oil over medium to high heat, about 8 minutes on each side. Take the legs out with tongs and reserve them, and pour the cooked oil out of the pot. Cook the onions in the remaining 1 tablesoon oil over medium heat until it turns translucent, about 10 minutes. Return the duck to the pot and pour the chicken broth over it. Simmer gently, covered, for 1 hour.

Slice the white section of the lemongrass stalks as fine as you can and add the slices to the duck, along with the galangal and the lime leaves. Simmer gently for 30 minutes more. Put two duck legs in each heated soup plate or bowl. Add the rest of the ingredients to the pot and stir to combine. Briefly bring to a simmer and season to taste. (If the broth needs salt, use more fish sauce instead—it's very salty and adds savor.) Ladle the curry broth over the duck and serve immediately.

Crispy Sweet-and-Sour Orange Duck

*W*hether this dish exists in China I don't know, but the ingredients and techniques are all typically Chinese, and the finished dish is far more like Chinese food than like any other cuisine I know. Although the braising is accomplished much like the French-inspired recipe on page 36, instead of wine or broth, typical braising liquids in European cooking, this duck is braised with broth that's been flavored with garlic, scallions, ginger, star anise, a little sugar, and Sichuan peppercorns. Sichuan peppercorns are to the Chinese what black and white peppercorns are to Westerners, but that's where the resemblance stops. They are always roasted before they are used, fortunately a process you can perform ahead of time in big batches, and they release a beguiling, pungent aroma vaguely reminiscent of burning leaves, but spicier. Once you start using them, they can become a habitual seasoning, especially when coupled with ginger, garlic, and something sweet. Star anise is easy to recognize because it's shaped like a star; each of the star's spikes contains tiny, black, very aromatic seeds. The flavor is similar to anise seeds, but it has a more pungent licorice-like aroma.

Because this duck takes several (albeit leisurely) hours to make, I usually prepare it for at least six. Although this recipe is somewhat involved—you're braising and then frying—the duck can be braised and the sauce (minus the scallions) prepared a couple days ahead of time. Only the frying must be done at the last minute. If you've refrigerated the duck, allow it to come to room temperature before frying or it won't get hot inside.

MAKES 6 MAIN-COURSE SERVINGS

9 Pekin (Long Island) duck legs, including both drumsticks and thighs
3 juicing oranges
¼ cup dark soy sauce, preferably a Japanese brand
2 cloves garlic, peeled and chopped
Three ¼-inch-thick slices fresh ginger
6 star anise (available in Asian groceries), crushed
1 tablespoon sugar, or more to taste
1 tablespoon Sichuan peppercorns, roasted in an iron skillet
  over medium heat for 10 minutes until they smell fragrant (see page 98)
3 tablespoons rendered duck fat (see page 15), peanut oil, or vegetable oil, for sautéing
5 cups brown duck broth (see page 8), chicken broth (see page 10), or water
6 cups peanut or vegetable oil, for deep-frying
¾ cup cornstarch
3 scallions, including the greens, sliced fine
2 tablespoons balsamic vinegar, or more to taste

Separate the legs into drumsticks and thighs by slicing diagonally where the drumstick joins the thigh. Don't get frustrated; it takes some trial and error to find the joint where the two meet.

Trim the zest off the oranges with a vegetable peeler. Cut the strips of zest from one of the oranges into fine julienne (very thin little strips), transfer to a small fine-mesh strainer, and plunge the julienned zests into boiling water for 2 minutes to eliminate bitterness. Rinse them under cold running water and reserve. Do the same thing with the strips of zest, keeping the julienned zests and strips separate. Squeeze the oranges into a small bowl and add the strips of orange zest, the soy sauce, garlic, ginger, star anise, sugar, and roasted Sichuan peppercorns.

Pat the duck parts dry, heat the duck fat in a heavy-bottomed pot over medium heat, and sauté, about 12 minutes on each side, until they are well browned. Using tongs, gently remove the duck from the pot and pour out and discard the cooked fat. Put the duck back in the pot with the orange mixture and broth or water, and bring to a simmer over high heat. As soon as the liquid reaches a simmer, cover the pot and turn the heat down to low so the liquid is barely simmering—just a bubble or two will come up to the surface every few seconds. Continue simmering for 2 hours.

Gently transfer the duck parts to a plate with tongs. If you like, hack off the ends of the drumsticks with a cleaver or chefs' knife first. Strain the braising liquid through a fine-mesh sieve into a clean saucepan. Bring it to a gentle simmer, with the saucepan set off-center over the heat source so the broth bubbles only on one side and pushes the fat over to the other side. Skim off any fat and scum with a small ladle. Continue simmering and skimming until you're left with 1½ cups braising liquid, and reserve.

Preheat the oven to 350°F.

Heat the 6 cups oil for frying in a large heavy-bottomed pot—the oil should come only about a third of the way up the sides of the pot or it might boil over. Stir the cornstarch together with ¾ cup water. When the oil reaches 335°F, roll the duck in the cornstarch paste, one piece at a time, then gently lower it into the oil with a frying spider or slotted spoon. (If you don't have a deep-fry thermometer, the oil is ready when you put a small chuck of duck meat into the oil and it is immediately surrounded with bubbles and floats.) Deep-fry the duck, six pieces at a time, for about 5 minutes each, until the skin is golden-brown. Work in batches, reserving the fried duck in a hot oven on a plate or sheet pan lined with paper towels to absorb excess oil. Adjust the oil temperature, if necessary, to ensure that the duck is evenly browned but not too dark after the 5-minute cooking time.

While the duck is frying, bring the reduced braising liquid to a simmer and stir in the scallions, reserved julienned orange zest, and balsamic vinegar. Season to taste with more vinegar and more sugar if necessary. If the sauce needs salt, add a little more soy sauce instead.

Put three pieces of duck in each soup plate, spoon 4 tablespoons sauce over each, and serve.

Pappardelle with Duck Sauce

I've always been fascinated by the interrelatedness of foods and especially by the relationship between sauces and soups, stews and braising liquids. The genius behind Italian sauces such as Bolognese sauce and duck sauce is that the solid parts of a stew are chopped or shredded and incorporated into the sauce itself. Because a relatively small amount of sauce can be used to give a full, rich flavor to pasta, a little bit goes a long way. If you cook duck breasts with any regularity, save the legs in the freezer and when you have enough to make it worth the effort— at least six—go ahead and make a batch of this sauce. If you want, make a double recipe and freeze the extra— it keeps for months. You can also enhance the sauce by making a broth out of the duck carcasses, reducing it, and using it, along with the wine and tomatoes, to braise the legs.

In Tuscany duck sauce—*salsa alla anatra*—is served with pappardelle, which are like fettuccine except they're ½ inch wide, but you can serve it with virtually any pasta you like. I provide a recipe for fresh pappardelle, but packaged pasta is great too. In Italy pasta is never served as a main course but as a first or second course after antipasti.

MAKES 5 CUPS SAUCE, ENOUGH FOR 6 FIRST-COURSE OR LIGHT MAIN-COURSE SERVINGS
OR 4 SUBSTANTIAL MAIN-COURSE SERVINGS

6 duck legs, including both drumsticks and thighs
Salt and pepper
2 to 6 tablespoons rendered duck fat (see page 15), butter, or olive oil, as needed
1 large carrot, peeled and chopped fine
½ stalk celery, chopped fine
1 large onion, peeled and chopped fine
4 cloves garlic, crushed, peeled, and chopped coarse
2 cups white wine
2 cups brown duck broth (see page 8) or chicken broth (see page 10)
2 pounds ripe tomatoes (about 6 medium), peeled, seeded, and chopped,
  or one 28-ounce can whole tomatoes, seeded and chopped (see page 59)
1 bouquet garni (3 sprigs thyme, 3 sprigs parsley, and 1 imported bay leaf,
  tied together with kitchen twine)
1 recipe homemade pasta dough (see page 60), or
  12 ounces dried pappardelle or fettuccine
½ cup all-purpose flour (if you're making fresh pasta)
1 tablespoon olive oil

TO SERVE
2 cups freshly grated Parmigiano Reggiano

Season the duck legs with salt and pepper. Melt 4 table-spoons of the duck fat in a heavy-bottomed pot and brown the duck legs over medium to high heat, about 8 minutes on each side. If you can't fit them in the pot in a single layer, brown them in batches. If the fat in the pot begins to smell burned, pour it out and replace it with 2 tablespoons new fat. Reserve the duck legs. Add the carrot, celery, onion, and garlic to the pot and stir them in the fat over medium heat for about 10 min-utes, until they barely begin to brown. Pour in the wine, broth, and tomatoes, and nestle in the bouquet garni. Put the duck legs, skin side up, back in the pot, along with any juices that have run out onto the plate. Don't worry if all the legs aren't submerged in liquid.

Bring to a boil over high heat, then turn down to low to maintain a gentle simmer. Cover the top of the pot with a sheet of aluminum foil and press the foil down in the center. (This is so the legs not covered with broth are basted on the inside of the pot.) Cover the pot and let it stew for 2 hours. Check the legs after 10 minutes to make sure they're at a low simmer—a bubble should rise gently to the surface every couple of seconds—and adjust the heat accordingly.

If you're using homemade pasta, roll the pasta dough in sheets as shown on page 60. Roll the sheets up—keep the rolls loose so the pasta doesn't stick to itself—and slice the rolls into ½-inch-wide strips. Toss the strips with flour to keep them from sticking together and heap them in a loose mound.

Use a pair of tongs to gently transfer the legs to a dish, then strain the braising liquid through a fine-mesh sieve into a small saucepan. Discard the bouquet garni. Work the aromatic vegetables through a food mill or a strainer with the back of a ladle and add the puree to the braising liquid. Set the saucepan, a bit off-center, over low to medium heat so the liquid boils up on one side only. Use a small ladle or spoon to skim off any fat or froth that rises to the surface on the opposite side from where the liquid is boiling. Continue reducing and skimming for about 30 minutes, until the liquid has reduced by half and you've skimmed off most of the fat. You'll end up with about 2 cups of reduced braising liquid.

While the braising liquid is reducing, pull the fatty skin off the duck legs and discard it. Pull away the meat in shreds and coarsely chop it—it should be a bit coarser than hamburger meat. When the braising liquid is ready, stir in the duck meat. Season to taste with salt and pepper.

Just before you're ready to serve, cook the pasta in boil-ing salted water with the 1 tablespoon olive oil—about 2 minutes for fresh pasta and according to the direc-tions on the package for dried. Drain the pasta in a colander and toss it in a bowl with half the sauce. Spoon it into wide heated soup plates, spoon the rest of the sauce over it, and serve. Pass the grated cheese at the table.

Peeling and Seeding Tomatoes

Peel fresh tomatoes by plunging them in boiling water for 30 seconds and immediately rinsing them off under cold water. Pull away the skin with your thumb and a paring knife. You can seed them in one of two ways. If you need wedges, as for a salad, cut the tomato in half from top to bottom and then slice each half into the number of wedges you want. Push the seeds out of each wedge with your thumb. If you're chopping the tomatoes, cut the tomatoes in half through the equator and squeeze each half in the palm of your hand until the seeds squirt out. Chop the halves.

If you're using canned tomatoes, which are already peeled, drain them in a colander—I don't bother saving the liquid in the can—and dig your thumb into the side of each tomato to release the seeds. Squeeze out and discard the seeds.

Homemade Pasta Dough

MAKES ALMOST 2 POUNDS, ENOUGH FOR 6 TO 8 SERVINGS

3 cups all-purpose flour
4 large eggs
1 tablespoon olive oil
Flour or water, for kneading

Combine the flour, eggs, and olive oil in a stand-up mixer and work the mixture until it has the texture of coarse sand. (If you don't have a stand-up mixer, knead the ingredients together by hand or in a food processor.) When you pinch some of the mixture it should hold together. Pour it out onto the work surface and knead it with the heel of your hand until it forms a ball. (You may need to sprinkle it with water if it won't come together or knead in a little flour if it feels sticky.)

Set up pasta machine, adjust it to the thickest setting, and feed manageable amounts of dough through the rollers (about ½ cup at a time), folding the flattened dough over itself between rollings until it's well-kneaded and feels like suede. Sprinkle the dough with flour as you work to keep it from sticking to the machine. Roll it through the rollers, setting the rollers one notch closer together after each rolling. If the sheets of dough become long and unwieldy, cut them in half crosswise. Continue rolling until the pasta is very thin—but not so thin you can see through it— finishing with the last or next-to-last setting on the machine. If you're not using the pasta right away, spread it on well-floured sheet pans and cover it with plastic wrap to keep it from drying out.

RIGHT, TOP TO BOTTOM: *1. Combine all ingredients, except extra flour or water, in a standup mixer with paddle blade. 2. Work mixture until it has texture of coarse sand. 3. Roll out dough in pasta machine as described above.*

Roasting

IF YOU'RE LUCKY ENOUGH to get hold of a wild duck, or if you're in Europe, where ducks are leaner, you can simply roast your duck at 500°F for 25 minutes (450°F for 35 minutes for a domestic wild duck) and it will end up with crispy skin and pink, medium-rare meat. If you cook an American domestic duck this way, you'll end up with raw flesh covered with a layer of flabby fat. American ducks must be cooked slowly, for a long time, so the fat contained in the skin has time to render. This, of course, means that you won't be able to have duck roasted to a pink medium rare but will have to settle for flesh that's cooked all the way through to well done. The payoff is that the skin will be crispy and, despite the long cooking time, the flesh will be moist because it's been well protected by the fatty skin. Because slow-roasting duck bastes itself as it cooks in its own fat, the result is much more like confit—meltingly tender flesh with crispy skin—than it is like, say, roast chicken.

When roasting whole duck, score the breast skin in two directions, as you do when sautéing (see page 12), so that the fat renders more completely out of the skin. As the duck roasts, it will release juices that will collect under the fat in the roasting pan. If you notice that these juices are caramelizing and threatening to burn, add half a cup of water or broth to the roasting pan as often as necessary. If the duck itself is getting too brown, turn the heat down to 300°F. While I usually opt for cooking duck legs and breasts using different methods, there's nothing like the drama of a whole roast duck. Just keep in mind that the meat should be cooked through. Although the long cooking time I suggest for whole duck would dry out most meats, the duck stays moist because of the protective layer of fatty skin.

Whole Roast Duck

MAKES 4 MAIN-COURSE SERVINGS

1 Pekin (Long Island) duck (about 5 pounds)
Salt and pepper
1 cup brown duck broth (see page 8), chicken broth (see page 10),
  or water (see Note), or more as needed

Cut the wings off the duck where they join at the breast, then cut them through their joints into three pieces each. Make a series of about 20 diagonal slashes in the skin covering each duck breast. Be careful not to cut all the way down to the meat—you just want to expose the fat contained in the skin. Change directions and make another series of slashes perpendicular to the first. Thoroughly season the duck with salt and pepper.

Put the duck, breast side up, in a roasting pan, cast-iron skillet, or oval baking dish—the sides should be at least 2 inches high to catch the fat—and arrange the wing pieces around the duck. I use an old iron skillet for roasting duck, but any heavy-bottomed sauté pan that's large enough to hold the duck will do. Slide the duck into the oven and turn the temperature to 300°F—there's no need for preheating, since you want to give the duck time to render its fat.

When the duck has roasted for 1 hour, take it out of the oven. Spoon the rendered fat into a small bowl, leaving any juices in the bottom of the roasting pan. Smell the fat—if it doesn't smell burned, you can save it for cooking. If the juices have carmelized on the bottom of the pan and are threatening to burn, add ½ cup broth or water—and do this as often as necessary during the roasting. Turn the duck over, back side up, and roast it for 1 hour more, then turn it breast side up

again, raise the heat to 350°F, and roast the duck for 2 hours more.

The purpose of all these machinations is to end up with a duck with crisp skin and meltingly tender flesh. If you're unsure about the texture of the flesh, insert a skewer into a thigh—it should slide out with no resistance. The duck should look shiny, golden brown, and glazed. When it passes these tests for doneness, transfer the duck to a platter and keep it warm while you're preparing the *jus,* or cooking juices.

Pour the fat and any juices left in the roasting pan into a glass pitcher or fat separator. If the juices accumulate under the fat in the pitcher, just let the fat rest for 10 minutes, then spoon or ladle off the fat and discard. If the juices have caramelized on the bottom of the roasting pan instead, stir in ½ cup broth or water, set the roasting pan on the stovetop, and scrape the bottom of the pan with a wooden spoon to loosen the caramelized juices. Transfer the duck to a cutting board and carve the duck at the table. Spoon or pour a couple tablespoons of the juices over each serving.

NOTE: If you've braised duck thighs recently, you can substitute the reserved braising liquid. Cook it down to ½ cup before adding.

CARVING A DUCK

One of the beauties of a roast is the ritual of presenting it at the table and carving it in front of expectant guests. However, you may want to practice by yourself in the kitchen, or in front of family or close friends, until you become adept.

Set the duck on a cutting board with the legs facing you on a diagonal from the left. (If you're left-handed, it will be on a diagonal from the right.) Holding the duck still with a fork, slide a long, thin carving knife between the leg closest to you and the breast; cut all the way through to where the leg bone joins the duck's back. Cut through the joint and remove the leg by cutting along the back, carefully leaving any meat attached to the leg and not the back. Put the leg on the cutting board and cut diagonally where the drumstick joins the thigh, separating the two.

Next, slide the knife along the breastbone, keeping it pressed against the bone, until you've cut all the way down to the cartilage. Keeping the knife flush against the cartilage, slide it under the breast until the breast comes away. Separate it from the rest of the duck and place it, skin side up, on the cutting board.

Turn the duck around and repeat on the other side. Slice the breast and cut the meat off the thighs and drumsticks. Give everyone a little of each, on heated plates. Spoon or pour a couple tablespoons of the juices over each serving.

RIGHT, CLOCKWISE FROM TOP: *Crêpes, Chinese plum sauce, shredded scallions, shredded duck meat, and crispy duck skin.*

Peking Duck

$\mathcal{M}$any people are disappointed by their first Peking duck dinner because the crispy skin, which is the best part, is usually served first, wrapped with a scallion in a little pancake and dipped in plum sauce. The rest of the duck, the meat, is served next and is a bit of an anticlimax. I avoid this problem by serving the meat and skin together, so my guests can use them both in their little pancakes. If you want to serve just the skin, serve it as a first course and use the meat in the shredded duck salad on page 141.

Making Peking duck is a bit involved, a process requiring a bicycle pump according to most recipes—just enough to cause most of us to turn the page. Fortunately you can get perfectly satisfying results without the pump. Basically Peking duck is a slow-roasted whole duck that's been marinated with a spicy sweet-and-sour mixture. To help stiffen and dry the skin, the duck is immersed a number of times in boiling water and dried after each dipping. (A hair dryer is helpful to speed up the drying process.)

MAKES 4 TO 6 MAIN-COURSE SERVINGS

1 Pekin (Long Island) duck (about 5 pounds)
1 teaspoon Chinese five-spice powder
¼ cup honey
2 tablespoons grated fresh ginger
2 tablespoons balsamic or sherry vinegar
3 tablespoons dry sherry

TO SERVE
1 recipe Chinese crêpes (see page 69)
12 scallions
2 cucumbers
1 cup Chinese plum sauce

BELOW, LEFT TO RIGHT: *Before roasting your Peking duck, brush the whole duck with glaze, as shown in the first photo, and hang it to dry for an hour. When taking the skin and meat off of the roasted duck, as illustrated in photos 2 through 5, do your best to leave the skin intact. See recipe for detailed instructions.*

To dry the skin: Put about 8 quarts water—enough to completely cover the whole duck—in a large pot and bring it to a rapid boil. Submerge the duck in the water for 1 minute, then take it out and hang it. (I tie a string around one of its wings and attach the other end of the string to the middle of a rolling pin. I then set the rolling pin on two chairs so the duck is suspended between them during the drying.) Let the duck dry for 1 hour, or if you're in a hurry, use a hair dryer to dry it in about 5 minutes. Repeat this process three more times.

To glaze: In a saucepan, combine the five-spice powder, honey, ginger, vinegar, and dry sherry with ½ cup water, briefly bring to a boil, and let cool. Brush the duck thoroughly with the honey mixture and hang it to dry again for about 1 hour, or if you prefer, use a hair dryer to dry it in about 5 minutes. Repeat two more times for a total of three times.

To roast the duck: Put the duck, breast side up, in a roasting pan or oval baking dish, turn the oven to 300°F—there's no need for preheating—and roast the duck for 4 hours, turning it over after each hour so it roasts evenly. After 2 hours, raise the temperature to 350°F. If you have any of the honey mixture left, brush it on the duck as it's roasting. If at any point the skin starts to get too dark—it should be the color of maple syrup—cover the area with aluminum foil.

While the duck is roasting, cut the scallions in half lengthwise so you end up with 24 thin strips. Peel the cucumbers and slice them as thin as you can—a plastic vegetable slicer or a mandoline comes in handy here.

To cut up the duck: Cut the skin and meat away from the duck in one piece by sliding a knife along the breastbone, keeping it pressed against the bone until you've cut all the way down to the cartilage. Keeping the knife flush against the cartilage, slide it under the breast until the breast comes away.

Cut through the leg joint, taking care not to cut the skin. Run the tip of the knife through the joint where the leg bone attaches to the rest of the duck. Cut the meat away from the bone, working from the inside. You will have to cut the end of skin that is attached to the end of the bone.

Turn the duck on its side and remove the rest of the skin and any meat off the back. Disjoint the wings from the wishbone. Once you've reached the center of the back, flip the duck back so the breastbone is again facing up. Remove the opposite breast and leg using the same method as before. Keep cutting around the center carcass until it is completely free from the meat and skin, and discard it.

Cut the skin into strips about 3 inches long and 1 inch wide. Cut the meat away from the bone as neatly as you can, and serve both the meat and the skin on a heated platter.

Pass the pancakes and plum dipping sauce along with the duck. Demonstrate by picking up a pancake, putting in a strip of skin, a couple of strips of meat, half a scallion, and a cucumber slice or two and rolling it up. Dip in the plum sauce and eat with your fingers.

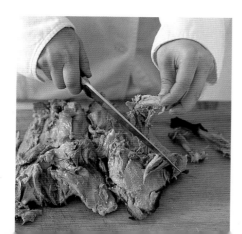

Chinese Crêpes

*R*ecipes for the pancakes traditionally served with Peking duck are frighteningly complicated. I cheat and make a simple crêpe batter flavored with a little sesame oil. To make these small pancakes, you need a 6- or 8-inch sauté pan, preferably nonstick or seasoned cast iron. If you want a cheap but effective pan, buy a cast-iron skillet at a hardware store. With a little practice and enough pans, you can make more than one crêpe at a time.

MAKES 24 CRÊPES OR MORE

1 cup all-purpose flour
2 large eggs
1½ cups water
¼ teaspoon salt
2 teaspoons dark sesame oil, preferably a Japanese brand
Vegetable oil, for the pan

In a mixing bowl, combine the flour, eggs, and enough of the water to produce a smooth paste. Gently whisk in the rest of the water and the salt and sesame oil. Strain the mixture through a fine-mesh sieve to eliminate lumps.

Brush a pan with vegetable oil—you need only a very thin coating—and ladle in just enough batter to cover the bottom of the pan. Lift the pan and tilt it so the batter completely covers the bottom. Pour any excess batter back in the mixing bowl. (After a few crêpes, you'll figure out exactly how much batter you need.)

Cook the crêpe over medium heat for about 3 minutes, until it starts to curl up at the edge. Using both hands, pick up the crêpe using the side opposite from you and flip it over. (You can use a spatula instead, but I find the finger technique easier.) Cook for 1 minute more.

As you make the rest of the crêpes, spread them out on a sheet pan covered with wax paper—don't just stack them or they'll stick together. If you want to freeze them for later use, put a piece of wax paper between each crêpe, then wrap the whole package in plastic wrap and again in aluminum foil.

NEAR LEFT: *Rolling pieces of duck skin, duck meat, scallions, and cucumbers in a Chinese crêpe.* FAR LEFT: *Peking duck and scallions— wrapped in crêpes and ready to eat. Dip them in plum sauce.*

Slow-Roasted Duck Legs

Although the preceding recipes for whole roast duck (see page 63) and Pekin duck (see page 66) are succulent, I rarely bother roasting a whole duck because it requires such long cooking time that it's easy to overcook the breast meat if you're not careful. Roasting duck legs, however, is a totally different matter. When cooked rare, the meat on a duck leg is too tough, but when slow-roasted until the meat is well-done, most of the fat is rendered out of the leg, the meat has a moist and melting texture, and the skin is crisp and juicy.

One of these slow-roasted legs makes a light main-course serving. For a more substantial main course, serve them at the same time as the breasts: You can give everyone one duck leg plus a little less than one Pekin duck breast or a little less than half a mullard breast. You can also pull the roasted leg meat and skin off the bones and toss them in a salad, or use the meat for the spring rolls on page 85.

The easiest way to use leftover duck legs is to roast them slowly, until they render their fat. Simply place them, skin side up, in a roasting pan or ovenproof skillet just large enough to hold them in a single layer, and bake them for 2 hours at 350°F—no need to preheat the oven. Pour out and discard the fat, which will be too cooked to save.

Serve the roasted duck legs plain or with one of your favorite sauces or salsas. You can also substitute slow-roasted duck legs for slowly simmered ones in one of the recipes in this book.

Slow-Roasted Duck Legs with Hoisin-Orange Glaze

*A*ll of us know that duck is good with orange, but when naturally sweet hoisin sauce is added, along with a little sesame oil, the duck legs take on a lovely exotic flavor with a little bit of sweetness.

MAKES 6 LIGHT MAIN-COURSE SERVINGS

6 Pekin (Long Island) duck legs, including both thighs and drumsticks
6 tablespoons hoisin sauce
6 tablespoons Grand Marnier, or other orange liqueur such as Cointreau or Triple Sec
2 teaspoons dark sesame oil, preferably a Japanese brand

Put the duck legs, skin side up, in a roasting pan just large enough to hold them in a single layer and roast them at 350°F. There's no need for preheating; you want to give the duck legs time to render their fat.

After they've cooked for about 1½ hours, combine the hoisin sauce, Grand Marnier, and sesame oil, and brush the glaze onto the skin side of the legs. Brush the legs with the glaze three more times, every 5 minutes or so, until you've used all the glaze and the duck has roasted about 2 hours total. Serve with rice or your favorite vegetable.

VARIATION: For Pekin duck legs, roast the duck legs as described above, but substitute the Peking duck glaze on page 66 instead.

Slow-Roasted or Braised Duck Legs with Sauerkraut

*S*auerkraut, like sweetbreads, anchovies, and cilantro, is a food that you either love or hate. No one is indifferent to it. I'm fortunate to love it, especially when it's served with rich meats—its tangy acidity and slightly crisp texture make the perfect foil. Sauerkraut is fantastic with duck confit (page 76), but here I suggest serving it with slow-roasted duck legs. Saurkraut is also great served alongside duck sausages, sliced or left whole, depending on their size.

MAKES 8 MAIN-COURSE SERVINGS

1 cup brown duck broth (see page 8), chicken broth
  (see page 10), or water (see Note)
Two 1-pound bags sauerkraut, drained in a colander and rinsed
8 whole slow-roasted or braised duck legs (see pages 70 and 36)
Salt and pepper

Put the broth or water and sauerkraut in a heavy-bottomed pot and bring to a gentle simmer. Place the duck legs—leave the fat behind in the roasting or braising pan—on top of the sauerkraut, cover the pot, and cook over low heat for 30 minutes. Reserve the duck legs in a bowl, and season the sauerkraut with salt and pepper to taste. Scoop the sauerkraut onto heated soup plates and place a duck leg, skin side up, on top of each serving.

NOTE: If you've braised duck thighs recently, you can substitute the reserved braising liquid. Cook it down to ½ cup before adding.

Confit

Confit

DUCK CONFIT IS MADE by gently cooking duck parts completely submerged in their own fat. Twenty-five years ago, confit could be found only in Southwest France, where it was used as a method of preserving duck and goose without refrigeration, but now the dish shows up more often than not in a typical French restaurant. Of all the ways to cook duck legs, confit is the most popular and fashionable. However, because duck confit recipes call for a lot of duck fat, many home cooks are horrified when they read the recipe. Keep in mind, though, that you'll end up eating very little of this fat, because it's rendered during the slow cooking.

Other than duck legs, duck fat is the only ingredient essential to making *confit de canard*. Fortunately our Long Island ducklings (Pekin ducks) have plenty of fat. A whole duck should provide enough fat to make confit out of its legs. I also save up duck fat in the freezer when making other duck dishes; simply trim off any pieces of raw fatty skin and freeze them in a tightly sealed plastic bag. When you've saved about 4 cups of fat, you're ready to make confit.

You can also buy eight whole ducks, which will give you enough fat and the sixteen legs to make the basic confit recipe that follows; you can tightly wrap the leftover breasts and freeze them for impromptu dinners. You should take all the fat and skin off the duck—except the skin covering the breasts and legs. The recipe makes more than you'll probably need at one sitting, but I think it's worth making a large batch and having some on reserve. However, cutting apart eight ducks takes time, so feel free to make less.

STORING CONFIT

I keep my confit in the refrigerator as an added precaution, where it will last for weeks or even months—and even longer in the freezer. While I once refrigerated it for over a year, it's something I don't dare recommend. If you want to store confit for longer than a week, make sure the glass jars you put it in are sterilized before you fill them. (Boil them for 10 minutes, or simply sterilize by placing them in a dishwasher in high heat. Spoon the confit into the jars while it's still hot—if it's only warm you may introduce bacteria—and make sure there's enough fat in the container to completely cover the confit. Let cool and seal.)

Once you broach the confit, it's best to use it within 1 week, since you will have destroyed the protective seal of fat. Because of this, I store confit in relatively small amounts—in 1-quart mason jars—so I'm not stuck using a lot at once. If you've broken into your confit and want to keep what's left in the jar from going bad, spoon the confit and its fat into a saucepan and bring to a gentle simmer for 10 minutes. Sterilize the jar as described above and put the confit and its fat back in the jar. If you're going to store them for any length of time, make sure all the confit duck legs are covered with fat and that none protrude out.

Duck Confit

MAKES 16 MAIN-COURSE SERVINGS, OR MORE WHEN
USED AS A COMPONENT IN ANOTHER RECIPE

*Duck legs from 8 Pekin (Long Island) ducks
    (16 legs total)*
2½ tablespoons freshly ground black pepper
¾ cup coarse salt
*7 cloves garlic, peeled, chopped fine, and crushed
    to a paste with the side of a chefs' knife*
1½ tablespoons chopped fresh thyme
*Gizzards and hearts from 8 ducks
    (if they come with the ducks, otherwise don't bother)*
*Fat and skin from the 8 Pekin (Long Island) ducks,
    not including the fat attached to the legs and breasts
    (about 16 cups before rendering), or 12 cups already
    rendered duck fat (see page 15)*

Leave the skin attached to the legs but remove any
excess fat that surrounds the meat. Combine the pepper, salt, garlic, and thyme and rub the mixture into the
duck legs, especially on the fleshy side, and onto the
gizzards and hearts, if using. Place the duck legs, gizzards, and hearts in a large nonreactive bowl, cover
them with plastic wrap, and refrigerate overnight.

If you haven't yet rendered the duck fat trimmings,
chop them by hand or in a food processor; the more
finely they are chopped, the more quickly they'll render their fat. Put the chopped fat in a large heavy-
bottomed pot over medium heat. You can use a flame
tamer to prevent the bottom of the pot from scorching.

Wipe excess seasonings off the duck legs and giblets
with a moist towel and nestle the giblets and legs, skin
side down, into the pot with the fat. Keep pressing the

LEFT, TOP TO BOTTOM: *1. Rub duck legs with
seasoning mixture the night before. 2. Chop
reserved fat and skin by hand, or as shown
here, in a food processor. 3. Purée fat to turn it
into a paste. 4. Reserve fat if you're not using
it right away, or transfer it directly to a heavy-
bottomed pot.*

duck legs and giblets into the pot. As the fat on the outside of the legs renders, it will soon cover all the legs and giblets. Raise the heat so the surface of the confit is boiling; this tells you that the water contained in the duck is being released and is evaporating. Cook the confit for 2 to 3 hours, until the fat is clear—which means all the moisture has been cooked out—and a knife stuck into one of the legs slides in and out easily. Be very careful not to overcook the confit by cooking out all the moisture and burning the fat. This shouldn't be problem if you take the confit off the heat as soon as the fat is clear and the confit is easily pierced with a skewer. If you're cooking at high altitudes, you will need to add ½ cup water to the simmering fat or the moisture will evaporate before the duck is cooked.

Transfer the legs and giblets to glass jars, or to bowls if you're going to use them in the next few days. Strain the fat remaining in the pot through a fine-mesh sieve and ladle it, while still hot, over the confit. If you're planning on storing the confit for a week or more, make sure the meat is completely covered with the fat—no pieces of meat should protrude above the surface. While the fat is still hot, poke into the confit with a chopstick or skewer to release any air bubbles that might be trapped between the layers. Although confit is a traditional method of preserving meat, just to be safe, screw the lids on the jars and keep them in the refrigerator (see Storing Confit, page 75).

VARIATION: One way to add flavor and excitement to your confit is to grill the confit duck legs just before serving. You can also give them a subtle smoky note by grilling them before you turn them into confit.

RIGHT, TOP TO BOTTOM: *5. Heat fat over medium to high heat until it partially renders, about 20 minutes. Be careful not to burn it. 6. Put duck legs in hot fat, skin side down. 7. Cook over gentle heat for 2 to 3 hours, until fat is clear. 8. Remove legs from fat and reserve.*

Duck Confit with Sorrel and Spinach

*R*aw sorrel looks a lot like spinach, but once you heat it in the hot cream, it turns a dull gray-green. It has a tangy acidity that makes it the perfect counterpoint to the rich confit. If you don't grow it or can't find it, use all spinach.

MAKES 6 MAIN-COURSE SERVINGS

Two 10-ounce bunches fresh spinach
1 pound sorrel, if available, or another 10-ounce bunch fresh spinach
6 confit duck legs (see page 76)
Salt
½ cup heavy cream
Pepper

Pull the stems off the spinach and sorrel by holding each leaf in one hand and peeling the stem away from the underside of the leaf; even the part of the stem that runs along the center of the leaf should be removed. Discard the stems and wash the leaves in a big bowl of cold water, then transfer to a clean bowl with your splayed fingers so any grit is left behind. Repeat until there's no sand or grit left in the bottom of the bowl.

Heat the duck legs, wrapped in aluminum foil, in an oven set at 350°F for 25 minutes or in a covered container in a microwave for 5 minutes.

Meanwhile, bring about 4 quarts water and a small handful of salt to a rapid boil in a pot. Add the spinach—pushing it into the boiling water with a wooden spoon—and leave it in the water for 30 sec-

onds or until it "melts." Immediately drain it in a colander, rinse under cold running water, then gently squeeze it in your hands to eliminate excess water. Don't blanch the sorrel or it will lose all its flavor.

Shortly before you're ready to serve, put the cream in a sauté pan and boil it down to about half over high heat. If you're using the sorrel leaves, stir them in and cook over high heat until the liquid they release evaporates, about 4 minutes. Add the blanched spinach and stir it for a minute or two to heat it through. Season to taste with salt and pepper.

Spoon a mound of the spinach-sorrel mixture into the center of each heated plate and place a confit duck leg on top. Serve immediately.

HOW TO SERVE CONFIT

Much of the time, duck confit is used as a flavoring for stews, soups, and casseroles, including the world's ultimate casserole, cassoulet (see page 80). A simple, hot confit duck leg is also delicious by itself, but because duck confit gives the impression of considerable richness, it's worthwhile to juxtapose it with something crunchy, a little bitter, or sour. Salad greens, especially those with a little bitterness like endive, are a marvelous complement and pretty to look at. Sorrel, when you can find it, is tangy and delicious cooked in just a little cream and served in a mound under the confit duck leg (see page 76). I sometimes combine the limited amount of sorrel I get out of my garden with fresh spinach. Hot lentils, made at the last minute with fresh chopped parsley and flavored with plenty of vinegar and butter, also provide an exciting contrast of texture and flavor to confit.

Cassoulet with Duck Confit

A cassoulet is really just a French version of baked beans. But what beans they are! Duck confit or braised duck legs are nestled into the beans, and the whole concoction is baked. Bread crumbs are sprinkled over the cassoulet as it bakes—and in traditional versions a goodly amount of duck fat, too. Once browned, the now crispy bread crumbs are gently spooned back into the cassoulet and more fresh bread crumbs are added. The result of all of this is a slightly crunchy texture from the bread crumbs juxtaposed against the melting texture of the slowly cooked beans. The flavor of the whole thing is of duck. This recipe calls for duck confit. If you want to make a somewhat less rich version, substitute braised duck legs (see page 36). The total cooking time for this cassoulet is about 2½ hours.

MAKES 12 MAIN-COURSE SERVINGS

2 pounds (4½ cups) dried white beans, such as borlotti, cannellini, or great Northern

1 pig's foot, halved lengthwise (ask your the butcher to do this; optional)

2 pounds boneless pork shoulder or butt, or if difficult to find,
    4 pounds pork shoulder chops

1 bouquet garni (3 sprigs thyme, 3 sprigs parsley, and 1 imported bay leaf,
    tied together with kitchen twine)

2 medium onions, peeled

2 whole cloves, stuck into one of the onions

1 large carrot, peeled and cut into 4 cylinders

4 cloves garlic, crushed and peeled, plus 1 clove garlic, peeled and left whole

6 cups brown duck broth (see page 8), chicken broth (see page 10),
    or water, or more as needed

1 teaspoon salt, or more to taste

12 confit duck legs (see page 76)

4 cups fresh coarse bread crumbs, made from 1 loaf dense-crumb white bread

1 raw or precooked duck sausage, 12 inches by 2 inches (see page 107), or store-bought
    garlic sausage (if the sausage is too long for your pot, cut it in half)

Rinse the beans and put them in a bowl with enough water to cover by at least 8 inches so that as they expand, they'll still be covered. Let soak for 12 hours or overnight. Drain and reserve.

If using, put the pig's foot halves in a pot, cover with cold water, and bring to a boil over high heat. Boil for 5 minutes, drain in a colander, and rinse thoroughly.

Cut the pork shoulder or butt into rectangular pieces about 2 inches long and about 1 inch thick and 1 inch wide. If you're using shoulder chops instead, cut the meat away from the bone, then cut the meat from each chop into two or three pieces. Put the meat in a heavy-bottomed pot with the optional pig's foot, bouquet garni, both the onions (including the one stuck with two cloves), carrot pieces, and the 4 cloves crushed garlic. Pour over enough broth or cold water—or a combination—to cover by 3 inches, and bring to a gentle simmer. Cook for about 15 minutes, skimming off any froth or fat that floats to the top. Cover the pot, turn the heat down to low, and cook for 1 hour.

Add the beans and enough broth or water to cover by 1 inch. Return to a simmer and cook the beans for 45 minutes, adding the 2 teaspoons salt after they have cooked for 20 minutes. Gently stir the beans with a wooden spoon once or twice, scraping against the bottom of the pot to make sure they're not sticking and scalding. If the beans start to run dry, add more broth or water.

With a pair of tongs, take out the pig's foot, onions, carrot pieces, and bouquet garni, discarding the veg-etables and bouquet garni. If you like, cut any of the gelatinous meat covering the pig's foot into ½-inch dice and stir it into the beans. Taste the beans—they'll be mealy, but don't worry—and season to taste, if need be, with more salt.

Preheat the oven to 350°F. Rub the inside of a large baking dish, large roasting pan, or one or more gratin dishes with the peeled garlic clove. With a slotted spoon, transfer half the beans, the pork, and any foot gelatin into the baking dish or roasting pan, leaving the liquid behind in the pot. Arrange the duck legs on top, then add the rest of the bean mixture, again leaving the liquid behind in the pot. Now ladle over enough of the bean-cooking liquid to come three quarters of the way up the sides of the beans, reserving any liquid you haven't used.

Spread the top of the cassoulet with about a third of the bread crumbs and slide it into the oven. When the cassoulet is bubbling and the bread crumbs have formed a crust, about 30 minutes, gently push the crust down into the beans with the back of a large spoon. Sprinkle the top of the beans with half the remaining bread crumbs and bake for 1 hour more, until a second crust has formed. If at any point the cassoulet seems dry and stiff, gently stir in 1 cup of the reserved bean-cook-ing liquid, or water if you run out of liquid. Push the crust into the beans as before. Nestle in the sausage (cut it into 4-inch lengths if it's too big for the pot), push-ing some of the beans to the side and folding some of the bean mixture over the sausage. Sprinkle with the rest of the bread crumbs and bake until a third and final crust has formed, about 1 hour more, then serve.

Rillettes

*T*his incredible mixture of duck confit and fat isn't served much outside of France, perhaps because the sight of all the fat sends a lot of us screaming. But if one dish can make you forget your diet, this is it. Once you have made the confit, rillettes are easy to prepare—just work together some shredded confit with some duck fat and spices.

MAKES 2 CUPS, ENOUGH FOR 8 FIRST-COURSE OR HORS D'OEUVRE SERVINGS

4 confit duck legs (see page 76)
⅔ cup rendered duck fat (see page 15), cool or at room temperature,
  plus additional for pouring over the finished rillettes, if desired
¼ teaspoon ground cloves
¼ teaspoon ground ginger
¼ teaspoon ground nutmeg
¼ teaspoon ground white pepper

TO SERVE
Toasted French country bread or crackers

Pull the skin off the duck legs and discard it. Pull the meat away in thin strips, then use two forks to shred the meat—it should be fine enough to spread on toast or crackers. Transfer to a mixing bowl, stir in the rendered fat, and work in the cloves, ginger, nutmeg, and white pepper.

Serve the rillettes cool or at room temperature in little individual crocks or 4-ounce ramekins. If you like, cover each ramekin with a tablespoon or two of fat—this will keep the rillettes from turning dark from air exposure.

VARIATION: Before using the confit duck legs in the rillettes, smoke them according to the directions for smoking duck breasts on page 94.

BELOW, LEFT TO RIGHT: *1. After removing meat from confit, use your fingers or two forks to shred it. 2. Stir spices and fat into shredded confit. 3. Unless you're serving rillettes right away, cover top of each ramekin with a thin layer of fat.*

Duck Rillettes Ravioli

*I*f you've made a large batch of rillettes, you can flavor it with Asian ingredients like ginger and sesame oil and turn it into wontons (see the duck wonton soup, page 127). Or you can take an Italian or French direction by adding fresh herbs—marjoram is my favorite—and turn it into ravioli.

MAKES 24 RAVIOLI, ENOUGH FOR 4 FIRST-COURSE OR LIGHT MAIN-COURSE SERVINGS

½ recipe homemade pasta dough (see page 60)
1 cup rillettes, cold (see page 83)
⅓ cup concentrated duck broth (see pages 8 to 9), chilled in the refrigerator until it gels (optional)
2 teaspoons chopped fresh marjoram, or 1 teaspoon chopped fresh thyme
2 tablespoons finely chopped scallions (use only an inch or two of the greens)
1 clove garlic, peeled, chopped fine, and crushed to a paste with the side of chefs' knife
Salt and pepper
½ cup all-purpose flour
2½ cups brown duck broth (see page 8) or chicken broth (see page 10)

Roll out the pasta dough according to the directions on page 60, but instead of slicing the noodles, leave the pasta in whole sheets. Combine the rillettes, gelled broth, herbs, and garlic, and season to taste, if necessary, with salt and pepper. Form the ravioli using one of the three methods below, toss them gently with flour, and spread them on sheet pans covered with wax paper. Don't stack them or they may stick. Refrigerate until needed.

Completely by hand: Cut the sheets of pasta into 48 squares with a 2-inch square pasta cutter or a knife, and place 2 teaspoons of the rillette mixture in the center of 24 of the squares. Brush the edges around the filling with water and place one of the remaining unfilled squares on top. Pinch all around to seal in the rillettes.

Using a ravioli mold: These rectangular frames have indentations for forming the ravioli. Lay a sheet of pasta dough over the frame and press down with the plastic insert to shape the ravioli. This creates indentations for putting in the filling. Brush the edges of the ravioli with water, add the filling, and cover with a sec-

ond sheet of pasta. Roll over the whole thing with a rolling pin to separate the ravioli. Pinch around the edges of the ravioli to make sure they're well sealed.

Using a pasta machine: Pasta machines come with ravioli attachments that crank out perfect ravioli by feeding in two sheets of pasta along with the filling. I, however, have never been able to manage this three-handed process by myself. You'll need someone to hold at least one of the sheets while you crank.

To cook the ravioli, bring a large pot of salted water to a boil over high heat, then lower the heat to keep the water at a simmer. In another pot, bring the duck or chicken broth to a simmer and season to taste with salt and pepper. Gently slide the ravioli into the simmering water and cook them—don't boil them or they'll pop open—for about 4 minutes. Bite into a corner of one to make sure they're done. Use a skimmer or slotted spoon to distribute six ravioli into each heated soup plate or bowl. Ladle the hot broth over the ravioli.

Duck Confit Spring Rolls

*V*ietnamese cooks make two kinds of spring rolls—the kind described here, in which the ingredients are cooked ahead of time and then the spring roll is served cold—and the deep-fried variety. While Vietnamese spring rolls usually contain shrimp and pork, the same technique works marvelously for duck confit or the meat pulled off slow-roasted duck legs.

To make spring rolls, you'll need rice paper, which is completely edible and comes in various sizes in thin translucent rounds. I use the 8- or 8½-inch size for most things, including these spring rolls. Rice paper is easy to find in Asian markets, but you can also order it by mail (see Sources, page 154). Rice paper is dipped in warm water a sheet or two at a time, which turns it from crisp to pliable in a matter of seconds. Many spring rolls contain rice vermicelli noodles, but you can get by without them. In Vietnam, both fresh and fried spring rolls are dipped in one of two delicious cold sauces: *nuoc cham,* the dipping sauce recipe given here that is based on fish sauce, and *nuoc leo,* which is based on peanuts.

MAKES 12 ROLLS, ENOUGH FOR 6 HORS D'OEUVRE OR SIDE-DISH SERVINGS OR 4 FIRST-COURSE SERVINGS

6 confit duck legs (see page 76) or slow-roasted
   duck legs (see page 70)
Pepper
Salt (optional)
1 clove garlic, peeled and chopped fine
¼ pound dried rice vermicelli noodles
Twelve 8½-inch rounds rice paper
12 small crisp lettuce leaves, such as Boston, Bibb, or romaine
1 cup bean or alfalfa sprouts (optional)
½ cup roasted peanuts, chopped coarse in a food processor or by hand
1 medium red onion, peeled and sliced thin
1 bunch cilantro, leaves only
1 bunch mint or basil, leaves only

FOR THE DIPPING SAUCE
½ cup Thai fish sauce
½ cup rice wine vinegar
Juice of 4 limes (about ½ cup)
2 tablespoons sugar
4 Thai chiles or 8 jalapeño chiles, stemmed, seeded, and chopped fine
2 cloves garlic, peeled, chopped fine, and crushed to a paste
   with the side of a chefs' knife

Heat the duck legs in the oven or microwave to make the meat and skin easier to get off the bones. Remove and discard the skin. Pull the meat away from the bones, shredding it as you go. Transfer the duck to a bowl, taste it, and season it with pepper and, if necessary, salt. Stir in the chopped garlic.

Soak the rice noodles in cold water for 40 minutes. Taste one to see if it has completely softened; if not, soak the noodles in warm water until they soften. Drain in a colander.

When you're ready to assemble the spring rolls, fill a bowl with room-temperature water. Dip the rice paper in the water, a sheet at a time, for about 30 seconds—until it becomes soft and pliable—and transfer it to your work surface. Place a lettuce leaf over the bottom half of each round, then sprinkle over some of the sprouts, if using, a few chopped peanuts, some onion slices, a small mound of duck, and a few strands of vermicelli noodles. It's all right if the lettuce leaf reaches to the outer edges of the rice paper, but don't pile the other ingredients all the way to the edge or the spring rolls will be hard to roll up. Sprinkle with some of the cilantro leaves, then tear the mint leaves into smaller pieces and sprinkle them over the spring roll.

Start to roll the rice paper into a cylinder. As soon as the part facing you is wrapped under the filling, fold in the sides, then finish rolling the spring roll into a cylinder. Repeat with the rest of the spring rolls. It's fun to get guests into the kitchen to help with the rolling, but if you are not serving the spring rolls right away, you can make them ahead of time, cover them tightly with plastic wrap, and keep them in the refrigerator for up to 4 hours.

Stir together all the ingredients for the dipping sauce in a small serving bowl. Cut the spring rolls in half crosswise—cutting at a 45-degree angle makes for a pretty effect—and serve them with the dipping sauce.

RIGHT, TOP TO BOTTOM: *1. Place lettuce leaf over bottom half of moistened round of rice paper. 2. Arrange remaining filling ingredients over lettuce leaf. 3. Roll up rice paper just enough to cover ingredients. 4. Fold in sides of rice paper and finish rolling spring roll.*

Duck Confit Enchiladas with Green Sauce

I've always been a fan of chicken enchiladas served with a tart tomatillo green sauce and dolloped with sour cream, but using duck confit or slow-roasted duck legs instead takes something already very good to new heights. Don't confuse tomatillos with green tomatoes; they're different creatures. Fresh tomatillos are easy to recognize because the "tomatoes" are each covered with a paperlike sheath. Canned tomatillos work fine if you can't find fresh.

MAKES 6 MAIN-COURSE SERVINGS

2 medium onions, chopped fine
3 cloves garlic, peeled and chopped fine
4 tablespoons rendered duck fat (see page 15)
3 pounds fresh tomatillos, or four 10-ounce cans tomatillos
½ cup brown duck broth (see page 8), chicken broth (see page 10), or water
1 bunch cilantro, leaves only
6 jalapeño chiles, stemmed, seeded, and chopped fine
12 small corn tortillas
12 confit duck legs (page 76) or slow-roasted duck legs (see page 70)
1 pint sour cream

Over medium heat, cook the onions and garlic in 2 tablespoons of the duck fat in a heavy-bottomed pot large enough to hold the tomatillos. If you're using fresh tomatillos, peel off the papery skin and cut the tomatillos in quarters. If you're using canned tomatillos, drain them in a colander and chop them coarse. When the onions and garlic turn translucent and fragrant, about 10 minutes, add the tomatillos to the pot. Pour the broth over the tomatillos, cover the pot, and simmer for 10 minutes to soften the tomatillos. Then remove the lid and cook the tomatillos over medium heat until you have a chunky sauce, about 15 minutes more. Finely chop the cilantro and stir it into the sauce, along with the chopped jalapeños.

Preheat the oven to 350°F. To soften the tortillas, melt the remaining 2 tablespoons duck fat in a sauté pan and gently heat the tortillas, one at a time, in the fat. Pull the skin off the duck legs and discard it, then pull the meat away from the bones, shredding as you go. Roll the shredded duck meat in the tortillas and arrange the tortillas in a baking dish just large enough to hold them in a single layer. Spoon over half the sauce, cover with aluminum foil, and bake the enchiladas for 15 minutes. Take off the foil and bake for 15 minutes more, until the sauce starts to bubble.

Reheat the remaining sauce. Put two enchiladas on each heated plate, spoon the remaining sauce over them, and pass the sour cream at the table.

Smoking

THOUGH SMOKING LARGE AMOUNTS of fish or meat requires expensive equipment and even a smokehouse, small pieces of meat such as duck breasts are easy to smoke on top of the stove. Smoked duck breasts are marvelous if cooked right, but they can present the same problems you'll encounter when grilling—the fatty skin renders, the liquid fat burns, and the finished duck tastes like soot. You can of course remove the duck skin and fat, but so much of the flavor is in the fatty skin that it seems a pity to do without. My own solution is to render the fat first in a sauté pan and immediately chill the duck breasts so they don't overcook. Then I smoke them. To tell when a sautéed duck breast is done, but not overdone, I stick a meat thermometer through the side into the center of the breast and wait until the temperature measures about 130°F.

While there are lots of ways to go about smoking, keep in mind that there are two basic methods—hot and cold. Hot-smoked foods are cooked as you smoke them, since the smoke itself is hot. Cold-smoked foods are exposed to cold smoke, so they aren't cooked during the process. This method is best for cured foods or foods that have already been cooked. It's far easier to hot-smoke than it is to cold-smoke because cold-smoked foods must be smoked far enough away from the heat source that they don't cook.

I use one of four devices to hot-smoke duck: a stovetop smoker, an improvised stovetop smoker made from a wok or pot with a lid, a large ovenlike smoker that I special-ordered, or a covered barbecue. All of these require wood chips or sawdust from flavorful wood such as mesquite, hickory, vine cuttings, or fruit tree woods like pear or apple. For smoking supplies, see Sources, page 154.

The suggestions and methods for smoking given here are for duck breasts. You can also smoke duck legs using the same methods, but they must be precooked first. Use braised, slow-roasted, or confit duck legs (see pages 36, 70, or 76). Unlike duck breasts, which can dry out in a hot smoker, it's very hard to overcook the duck legs during smoking, since in a sense, they're overcooked already.

Stovetop-Smoker Method: This is a simple, inexpensive affair consisting of a stainless-steel rectangular box with a rack in it and a cover that slides on and off. All you do is put down some sawdust or wood chips and a sheet of aluminum foil (this is especially important if you're using sawdust; the foil keeps wood from getting on the food) and replace the cake-rack-like grill. You arrange the food on the grill, slide on the lid, and put the whole contraption on the stovetop. The temperature of the inside of the smoker can get quite hot, much like a very hot oven, but you can control the temperature somewhat by adjusting the stove.

Improvising a Stovetop Smoker: If you don't want to go out and buy a stovetop smoker, you can follow the method described in Barbara Tropp's marvelous book *The Modern Art of Chinese Cooking*. In order to pull it off, you'll need an old wok or heavy pot that you don't care about too much. I use a chipped enameled-iron Le Creuset pot, but an old-fashioned iron Dutch oven— usually inexpensive if you buy it at a hardware store—will also work. You'll also need a round wire cake rack as close to the size of the inside of the pot as possible and three empty thoroughly cleaned tin cans, all the same size, with both ends cut out, to raise the rack. The size can you need will depend on the height of the pot—I use cat food cans (tuna fish cans would also work) because my pot is rather low. If you're using a wok, you won't need the cans. Just make sure that the cake rack is the right size to hold the duck suspended above the wood chips or sawdust. If it's too large, you can use wire cutters to cut it to fit.

Line the bottom of the pot or wok with a double layer of heavy-duty aluminum foil. Put the wood chips or sawdust in the bottom of the pot, cover with another sheet of foil, insert the three cans, and set the cake rack on top of the cans. Open the windows for ventilation, put the pot on high heat, and let the wood chips or dust smoulder for a few minutes, until any strong acrid smell burns off. Turn the heat down to medium, arrange the pieces of duck on the cake rack, and cover the pot. Within 5 minutes, abundant smoke should be leaking out from under the lid. If you hear spattering and there's so much smoke that it starts to get scary, turn down the heat. If you see very little smoke (or no smoke) coming out from under the lid, turn the heat up.

Oven-Type Smoker Method: If you find yourself smoking a lot of foods, you may want to invest in an oven-type smoker. Mine is made of sheet metal, has racks in it just like an oven, and a hot plate on the bottom with a little pan designed for holding smouldering sawdust. It doesn't get as hot as a covered barbecue, so the smoking times tend to be somewhat longer—you'll have to check your duck by feeling its texture (it should just begin to feel firm instead of fleshy) or by cutting into a piece (it should be red to pink in the center). I set my smoker on medium to high and let the sawdust smoulder awhile—at first it has a rather strong, acrid smell that burns off in about 5 minutes— then I arrange the duck on the racks. (See Sources, page 154, for an oven-type smoker actually designed for smoking sausages.)

Covered Barbecue Method: This is probably the easiest way to hot-smoke duck. Build a fire in the barbecue as though you were grilling, but instead of spreading the hot coals evenly under the grill, heap them up on one side in the barbecue. Make sure the grill itself is perfectly clean, then brush it with olive oil.

Rub the fleshy side of the duck with olive oil. Put the wet wood chips on top of the coals and arrange the duck, flesh-side down, on the section of the grill that's removed from the coals. Cover the barbecue and smoke the duck for about 15 to 30 minutes (there may be a lot of variation in cooking times because the heat of the fire, the distance from the coals, and other factors vary). Serve immediately.

Brine for Grilled, Sautéed, or Smoked Duck

*M*any foods are improved by a short soak in a salt-and-sugar brine. Duck is no exception, especially since it always seems to work well with something slightly sweet.

MAKES ENOUGH BRINE TO CURE 6 PEKIN (LONG ISLAND) DUCK BREASTS OR 3 MULLARD BREASTS

2 cups fine salt
1 cup sugar
4 cups water

Combine everything in a nonaluminum pot and bring to a simmer. Stir to dissolve the salt and sugar.

Let cool at room temperature for 1 hour and then refrigerate until well chilled.

LEFT, CLOCKWISE FROM TOP: *Duck prosciutto, duck pastrami, duck rillettes, and duck sausage.*

Smoked Duck Breasts

6 Pekin (Long Island) duck breasts or 3 mullard breasts, skin on
Pepper

Use a knife to score the skin on the duck breasts in two directions, making about 20 slits per direction (see page 14 for more detailed instructions). Cut as deeply into the fat as you can without exposing the meat. Soak the breasts in the brine in the refrigerator—30 minutes for the Pekin duck and 45 minutes for the mullard.

To sauté the breasts: Drain, pat dry, and season the breasts on both sides with pepper. Heat a sauté pan over medium heat and cook the duck breasts, skin side down, over medium to high heat for 8 to 10 minutes for the Pekin duck and 12 to 18 minutes for the mullard. Check after 4 minutes to make sure the skin isn't burning—the sugar in the brine encourages burning—and if it is, turn down the heat.

While the ducks are cooking, chill a plate or sheet pan large enough to hold the duck breasts in a single layer in the freezer. When the breasts are ready, put them skin side down on the plate and transfer them to the freezer or refrigerator for 5 minutes to stop the cooking.

To smoke the breasts: Use one of the following techniques.

Wok method: Line a wok with a double layer of aluminum foil. Put ½ cup fruitwood, hickory, maple, or mesquite chips or sawdust (see Sources, page 154) in the bottom of the wok. Place a round wire cake rack in the bottom of the wok, put on the lid, and set the wok over high heat. Open the windows, and when smoke starts coming out from under the lid, quickly put the duck breasts on the cake rack and cover the wok again. Turn the heat down to medium and smoke the breasts—7 minutes for the Pekin duck breasts and 12 minutes for the mullard.

Pot method: Line an old heavy-bottomed pot with a double layer of aluminum foil and set a round wire cake rack on the bottom of the pot. If the cake rack is too big for the pot, cut out the outermost ring(s) with wire cutters. Remember, though, that the rack has to be big enough to hold the breasts in a single layer.

Take out the cake rack, spread ½ cup fruitwood, hickory, maple, or mesquite chips or sawdust (see Sources, page 154) on the bottom of the pot, and cover with another sheet of aluminum foil. Put the cake rack back in the pot, cover the pot, and put it over high heat. Open the windows, and when smoke comes out from under the lid, arrange the duck breasts, skin side up, on the rack, then cover the pot again. Turn the heat down to medium and smoke the breasts—7 minutes for the Pekin duck breasts and 12 minutes for the mullard.

Smoked duck confit: Smoke the confit duck legs in the same way as the breasts, but use lower heat and smoke them for at least 30 minutes. Serve the smoked confit as you would regular confit, or use it to make rillettes.

GLAZES FOR SMOKED OR GRILLED DUCK BREASTS

Smoked duck breasts are amazingly good with just a little seasoning, but if you like the flavor of orange with duck—a classic combination, of course—soaking the uncooked breasts in orange-flavored brine and then glazing them with cooked-down orange juice will do the trick. (To make the brine, heat the mixture on page 93 with some orange zest strips and cool before brining.) The teriyaki sauce on page 29 also makes an excellent glaze, brushed on while the duck is smoking.

Deep-Fried Duck

I've never had much luck with plain deep-fried duck. If deep-fried duck breasts render enough of their own fat, they're overcooked. The duck legs stay tough unless you fry them slowly and for a long time—in which case, you might as well go ahead and make confit (see page 76).

Deep-frying, however, is a marvelous technique for duck when combined with braising. Unlike sautéed or roasted foods, braised foods don't have that delightful crispy crust. But if you coat braised duck legs with a little cornstarch or flour and then deep-fry them, you'll get the best from each technique, leaving your duck with a melting interior and a crispy skin.

To deep-fry six braised duck thighs (see page 36), heat enough vegetable oil or pure (not extra virgin) olive oil to cover the thighs by an inch or two. The amount will of course depend on the size of your pot, but don't fill the pot more than half full with oil or it could bubble over.

Heat the oil to about 355°F, roll the thighs in cornstarch, and gently lower them into the oil, one at a time, with a spider (which looks like a spider's web with a handle) or a slotted spoon. You can tell the temperature is right if the thighs are immediately surrounded by bubbles. Fry until the thighs are golden brown and heated through, about 5 minutes. Serve with any sauce you'd use for sautéed duck breasts or braised thighs.

Duck Pastrami

*D*uck pastrami is much like regular beef pastrami, but with a deeper flavor and irresistible richness. Preparing it is a four-step process in which the duck breasts are first brined (plan ahead—this takes 4 days), then rubbed with spices and smoked. Following a preliminary gentle sautéing to rid the breasts of some of their fat, they are then braised to create pastrami. I like pastrami in a sandwich, but you can also put it on little toasts or crackers and serve it as an hors d'oeuvre.

MAKES 8 TO 12 SERVINGS

8 Pekin (Long Island) duck breasts or 4 mullard breasts
   (3 to 6 pounds total)

FOR THE BRINE
¼ cup Instacure No. 1 (see page 114)
5 cloves garlic, peeled and crushed
¼ cup powdered dextrose (see page 114)
⅔ cup noniodized salt
⅓ cup pickling spice (see page 114)

FOR THE SPICE MIXTURE
⅓ cup coriander seeds
3 tablespoons whole black peppercorns
⅓ cup paprika

FOR THE BRAISING LIQUID
2 medium onions, peeled and chopped
2 quarts brown duck broth (see page 8), chicken broth
   (see page 10), or water, or more as needed to cover
2 sprigs fresh thyme or ½ teaspoon dried
1 bay leaf, preferably imported (it's important not to use California
   bay leaves because they have an aggressive eucalyptus aroma)

In a large nonreactive bowl, combine all the brine ingredients with 5 quarts cold water, stirring until the powders dissolve. Add the duck breasts, making sure they're completely covered with brine, and refrigerate for 4 days.

Take the breasts out of the brine and pat them dry. To make the spice mixture, grind the coriander and peppercorns in a coffee grinder or blender, or crush them with a saucepan. Combine with the paprika and rub the spice mixture on both sides of the breasts.

Smoke the breasts as you would regular smoked breasts, but more slowly and over lower heat, for about 1 hour (see directions on page 94), until an instant-read thermometer stuck into the thickest part of the meat reads 125°F.

Score the breast skin in two directions as described on page 14 and sauté them, skin side down, over medium heat, 8 to 10 minutes for the Pekin duck breasts and 12 to 18 minutes for the mullard, checking every minute or two to make sure the spice mixture doesn't burn. (The idea is to render as much fat as possible without burning the spice coating.)

Put the breasts in a large heavy-bottomed pot with the onions, broth, thyme, and bay leaf. Bring to a gentle simmer, cover, and cook for 2 hours. Let cool completely.

Serve the pastrami sliced, as an hors d'oeuvre, or in sandwiches. If wrapped in plastic and refrigerated, it will last about 2 weeks.

Tea-Smoked Duck Breasts with Sichuan Pepper Marinade and Soy Glaze

These duck breasts are rubbed with ground Sichuan peppercorns before being glazed in the sauté pan with a mixture of sugar, soy sauce, balsamic vinegar, and sesame oil. After the glazing, the breasts are smoked with tea leaves or wood chips. Sichuan peppercorns, which you roast and grind yourself, give the breasts an inimitable flavor that enhances both the smokiness and the glaze. It's worthwhile to roast a whole 4-ounce bag of Sichuan peppercorns—they're easy to find at Asian grocery stores—grind them in a coffee grinder or blender, and then store them in the freezer. Roast the peppercorns in a heavy iron skillet over medium heat for about 15 minutes, stirring them every minute so they roast evenly. After grinding the roasted peppercorns, work the mixture through a fine-mesh strainer, regrind what doesn't go through the strainer, and strain again. Most of the work for this dish—the sautéing and glazing—can be done up to a day ahead of time.

MAKES 4 MAIN-COURSE SERVINGS

4 Pekin (Long Island) duck breasts or 2 mullard duck breasts
    (1½ to 2 pounds total)
2 tablespoons Sichuan peppercorns, roasted, ground, and worked
    through a fine-mesh strainer
1 tablespoon soy sauce
1 tablespoon sugar
1 tablespoon balsamic vinegar
1 teaspoon dark sesame oil, preferably a Japanese brand
¼ cup tea leaves or wood chips

Score the skin on the duck breasts as described on page 14 and rub them on both sides with the Sichuan pepper.

Sauté the breasts as described on page 14 but cook them for only 6 minutes on the skin side for Pekin breasts and 10 minutes for mullard breasts, then cook for 1 minute on the fleshy side. Transfer them to a plate, pour the cooked fat out of the pan, and add the soy sauce, sugar, vinegar, and sesame oil, stirring to combine. Bring the mixture to a boil over high heat and return the duck breasts to the pan, skin side down. Use a fork or a pair of tongs to move the breasts around for about 1 minute in the syrupy glaze. Turn the breasts over and repeat on the fleshy side, moving the breasts around until the glaze turns to a thick syrup, but stopping as soon as you smell the syrup start to caramelize.

Spread the tea leaves or wood chips in the bottom of an aluminum foil-lined wok or pot (see page 94 for details), or a stovetop smoker. Put the breasts in skin side up, and smoke them for 8 minutes from the point the tea leaves or wood begins to release smoke. Slice the breasts crosswise, at an angle, and serve them on hot plates. I like to serve these with a cucumber and yogurt salad, which makes a cool counterpoint to the spicy duck.

Curing

WHILE CURING WAS ORIGINALLY DESIGNED to preserve foods in the days before refrigeration, it also brings out flavors that makes it worth doing even if it's no longer important as a method for extending the life of perishable foods. Like pork, duck takes especially well to curing, and since duck is smaller, it can be cured much faster.

The simplest curing method consists of rubbing a duck breast with salt, pepper, and spices, wrapping it in a towel, and then hanging it in a cool place for two weeks. You can then slice it and serve it as though it were prosciutto. Duck can also be cured after it's chopped to make salami (see page 113), or it can be smoked and braised to make pastrami (see page 96).

Duck Prosciutto with Figs

Figs are a perfect match for duck prosciutto, as they are for regular prosciutto.

MAKES 6 FIRST-COURSE SERVINGS

One 1-pound mullard breast prosciutto (see page 101)
18 ripe fresh figs

Use a very sharp knife to slice the prosciutto as thin as you can. To serve, put three figs on each plate, and arrange the prosciutto slices around them.

Duck Prosciutto Carpaccio

I first read about this technique in Michel Guérard's book *La Cuisine Gourmande* (1977). The method for making duck prosciutto is essentially the same as the method for making prosciutto from pork, except that pork takes about a year to cure, and duck prosciutto, only two weeks. Make the duck version with the large mullard breasts, not with Pekin duck breasts, which are too small to cure properly.

MAKES 6 FIRST-COURSE OR HORS D'OEUVRE SERVINGS

10 juniper berries, crushed under a saucepan
2 tablespoons coarse salt
½ bay leaf, preferably imported, chopped
1 teaspoon coriander seeds, crushed under a saucepan
10 black peppercorns, crushed under a saucepan
1 clove garlic, peeled, chopped fine, and crushed to a paste
  with the side of a chefs' knife
One 1-pound mullard breast
1 black or white truffle (optional)
1 tablespoon very finely chopped chives
6 tablespoons extra-virgin olive oil

Combine the juniper berries, salt, bay leaf, coriander, peppercorns, and garlic in a small bowl. Spread half the salt mixture on a plate—preferably oval-shaped—just large enough to hold the mullard breast. Place the breast, fleshy side down, on top of the salt mixture and rub the rest of the mixture over the breast on the skin side. Cover with plastic wrap and let sit in the refrigerator for 24 hours. Pat dry and wrap tightly in a clean dish towel. Tie the dish towel at both ends with kitchen string, as though making a sausage, and hang the prosciutto in a cool, dry place for 2 weeks. (After 3 weeks, it will start to dry out.)

BELOW, LEFT TO RIGHT: *1. Rub duck breast with salt and spice mixture. 2. After curing, slice prosciutto. 3. Arrange in a serving dish, or serve with other cured duck products, such as duck pastrami, rillettes, and sausage.*

Within an hour before serving time, slice the duck prosciutto crosswise as thin as you can. If you're using the truffle, slice it very thin with a truffle slicer, a plastic vegetable slicer (the Benriner brand is my favorite), or a mandoline. Arrange the duck slices and, if you're using them, the truffle slices, together on individual plates. Combine the chives with the olive oil, lightly spoon the mixture over the slices, and serve.

VARIATION: If you're feeling ambitious, make a light duck *gelée* by whisking 2 cups good-quality cold duck broth—it should be gelatinous enough that it sets in the fridge—with 3 egg whites, a chopped small onion, and 5 sprigs fresh tarragon. Transfer to a small saucepan over high heat and, as soon as it approaches a boil, turn down the heat to maintain at a gentle simmer for 30 minutes.

Gently strain the hot *gelée* through a strainer lined with a triple layer of cheesecloth into a bowl containing the 1 tablespoon very finely chopped chives and the truffle if using. Cover with a plate and put it in the refrigerator until it sets, about 3 hours. Spread the *gelée* over the sliced prosciutto instead of the olive oil.

RIGHT: *Duck carpaccio with black truffles, chives, and olive oil.*

BUYING AND STUFFING SAUSAGE CASINGS AND PRECOOKING SAUSAGES

Cleaned and salted intestines (called casings) come in various sizes and can usually be bought in 1-pound tubs, enough for a lot of sausages. Hogs' intestines are for small- to medium-size link sausages and beef casings, called "beef middles," are for larger, salami-size sausages, about 2½ inches in diameter. You can ask your butcher to order the casings for you, or you can mail-order them (see Sources, page 154). Because sausage casings are usually packed with salt, they can be kept in the refrigerator for up to 1 year and don't take up much room—if they're not salted you can freeze them—and since they're inexpensive, it's worth stocking a small supply. You can also resalt casings that you've rinsed and keep them in the refrigerator—just be sure to use noniodized salt.

When you're ready to use the sausage casings, soak as many as you'll need in water for about 10 minutes, then, one at a time, fit one end of a casing on the kitchen tap and gently run cold water through it for about 30 seconds to eliminate salt. Start running the water slowly, so if the sausage casing has a crimp, you have time to unravel it before it bursts. Stuff the casings with a manual sausage stuffer (which looks like a giant syringe), a hand-cranked sausage stuffer (see photos below), the sausage-stuffing attachment on an electric mixer, or the sausage stuffer described below. Using the largest tube attachment, roll the length (or smaller piece) of casing up on the stuffing tube and begin feeding in the sausage filling—the mixer should be set on low speed or you should crank rather slowly.

BELOW, LEFT TO RIGHT: *1. Roll sausage casing onto tube that sticks out of meat grinder or sausage maker. 2. When using traditional sausage stuffer, shown here, push down on ground meat while cranking.*

When stuffing the casings, push the sausage meat into the casing so the sausage is firm and there are no air pockets. When you have a sausage the length you like—in this recipe 5 or 12 inches, depending on which casings you're using—turn off the machine and pull the sausage an inch or two away from the stuffing tube so you have some empty casing that you can twist to separate each sausage. Tie a knot around this empty space with a little piece of kitchen twine to form a sausage.

Whichever of the above methods you use to make sausage, the process is always a bit laborious. The results are so good that I think it's worth it, but if you find yourself making sausage often, you may want to order one of the special sausage makers from The Sausage Maker, Inc. (see Sources, page 154). They're shown in the catalog as heavy-duty arc-shaped tubes with rugged handles. They're very simple and efficient to use—more so than any of the other methods mentioned. Sausage casings, stuffers, and smokers can also be ordered from The Sausage Maker, Inc. (see Sources, page 154).

If you want to grill, sauté, or bake the links, poach them first. Gently place the sausages in a wide pan filled with cold water and bring to a gentle simmer. Don't let the water boil or the casings may tear. Depending on the thickness of the sausages, poach them for 30 to 45 minutes. If you have a smoker, you can smoke them for 2 hours without poaching them first—make sure they reach 180°F inside—following the directions on pages 91 to 92.

BELOW, LEFT TO RIGHT: *3. As sausage casing fills up, tie it into sections, depending on how long you want your sausages to be. 4. Hang sausages in smoker, or use one of the methods described on page 94, increasing cooking times as necessary, until sausages reach an internal temperature of 150°F. 5. The finished sausage.*

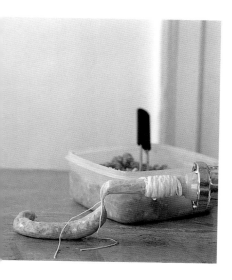

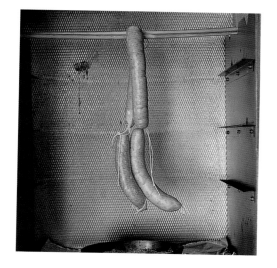

Duck Sausages

$\mathcal{W}$hen the collection of duck legs in my freezer gets out of hand, I make a simple version of duck sausages. The only part of the process that might be tricky is tracking down the right sausage casings and the fatback (unsmoked fatty bacon), both of which may have to be special-ordered by your butcher or from a mail-order source (see page 154).

With a food processor or meat grinder, I just grind the meat from the duck legs with fatback and, if I want to stretch the duck, some pork shoulder, season the whole thing with garlic, salt, and a four-spice mixture, and use my electric mixer with the sausage attachment to fill the sausages (see Buying and Stuffing Sausage Casings, pages 104 to 105). I sauté or poach the sausages and serve them with cooked lentils, red cabbage, sauerkraut, or with beans in a cassoulet (see page 110 or 44).

You can make your sausages as complicated or as extravagant as you like by adding cubes of duck breast, peeled pistachios, ham, prosciutto, and even diced truffles. The result is not only delicious but beautiful to look at when the sausages are sliced. When I make elaborate duck sausages, I sometimes bake them in brioche and serve a slice as an elegant first course (see page 111).

The exact size of your sausages may vary slightly from the amounts given below because of variations in the size of the casings and in how tightly you pack the sausages. I usually make my sausages from duck legs, but if you don't have legs saved up and want to start with whole ducks, you can use the breasts, too—with their fat trimmed off—and you can include some pork shoulder. For this recipe, you just need to come up with a total of 4 pounds meat.

Here are the equivalents:

4 to 5 Pekin (Long Island) duck breasts (skin removed and fat trimmed off) = 1 pound
3 to 4 Pekin (Long Island) duck legs (skin removed) = 1 pound

LEFT: *Duck sausages paired with a crock of green lentils.*

12 duck legs or the equivalent, per page 107
    (4 pounds meat total)
2 teaspoons salt
1 pound fatback, rind removed, chopped coarse
    to yield about 1 cup)
6 ounces chicken and/or duck livers (about 3)
2 large eggs
2 large cloves garlic, peeled, chopped fine, and crushed
    to a paste with the side of a chefs' knife
1 teaspoon finely chopped fresh thyme, or ½ teaspoon dried
2 teaspoons freshly ground black pepper
½ teaspoon ground cloves
½ teaspoon ground ginger
¼ teaspoon ground nutmeg
4 slices dense-crumb white bread, crusts removed
⅔ cup milk
2 tablespoons olive oil, or more as needed
7 feet of hog casings, or 4 feet of beef middles

Take the skin off the duck legs or breasts and save it in the freezer to render for cooking or making confit. Take the meat off the bone and cut it into chunks. Combine it with the salt, fatback, livers, eggs, garlic, herbs, and spices and grind the mixture together in a meat grinder or food processor until it has the consistency of hamburger meat. Soak the bread in the milk, break it up with your hands, and then work it into the duck mixture.

To test, make a tiny hamburger with the mixture and sauté it in olive oil over medium to high heat until it cooks through. Taste it and, if necessary, adjust the salt or other ingredients. Stuff the sausages—and precook if necessary—as described on pages 104 to 105.

OPPOSITE: *Duck Sausages with Red Cabbage (recipe on page 110).*

Duck Sausages with Red Cabbage

Cabbage is the perfect foil for rich, fatty things like sausage. You can serve your homemade duck sausages with sauerkraut (see page 72) instead, but this cabbage is sweet and sour and lightly crunchy, so you'll get much the same effect. Plus the dish looks beautiful.

MAKES 6 MAIN-COURSE SERVINGS

2½ pounds red cabbage (1 large head)
1 tablespoon coarse salt
2 Granny Smith apples, peeled and diced into ⅓-inch cubes
Juice from ½ lemon (about 1½ tablespoons juice)
1 large onion, peeled and chopped fine
3 medium carrots, peeled and sliced into ¼-inch-thick rounds
2 cloves garlic, peeled and minced
3 tablespoons rendered duck fat (see page 15) or butter
¼ cup cider vinegar, or more to taste
3 tablespoons honey
7 juniper berries, crushed under a saucepan
¼ teaspoon fennel seeds
1 cup brown duck broth (see page 8), duck leg braising liquid
  (see page 36), or chicken broth (see page 10)
2 precooked duck sausages, 10 to 12 inches long and 2 to
  2½ inches thick (see page 107)
Salt and pepper

Pull off any wilted leaves from the cabbage and cut the head into quarters through the root end. Slice off the section of core that runs along the edge of each of the four wedges and slice the wedges crosswise as fine as you can. Combine the shredded cabbage with the coarse salt and rub the salt with the cabbage until it's dissolved—until you don't feel the graininess under your fingers—then transfer the cabbage to a colander. Toss the apples with the lemon juice and reserve.

In a wide pot, cook the onion, carrots, and garlic in the duck fat over medium heat until the vegetables soften, about 10 minutes. In a colander, thoroughly rinse the cabbage with cold water and squeeze it, a small bunch at a time, in your fist as hard as you can to extract the salt and water. Add the cabbage to the vegetables and cook, stirring frequently, until the cabbage softens but is not mushy, about 20 minutes. Add the vinegar, honey, juniper berries, fennel seeds, and broth, stirring to combine, then nestle in the sausages. Cover the pot and simmer over medium heat, stirring gently every few minutes, for about 20 minutes—long enough to heat the sausages. Stir in the apples and cook for 5 minutes more, then season to taste with salt and pepper. Slice the sausages and arrange them with a mound of cabbage on heated plates.

Duck Sausage *en Croûte*

*I*n Lyon, thick sausages baked in a generous crust of brioche has long been a traditional dish. The buttery melting texture of the brioche (a bread that contains lots of butter and eggs) next to the sausage is one of the sublime combinations of the table. They use various sausages in Lyon—one place I know even uses foie gras—but here, of course, it's got to be duck sausage. If you're making sausages and planning to use one for this dish, use the thicker casings—the beef middles—and make at least one of the sausages 1 foot long. In this recipe, the brioche dough is prepared in stages, making it somewhat time-consuming but also giving it a deeper flavor than quicker versions. The brioche recipe is adapted from Julia Child's *Baking with Julia*.

MAKES 8 FIRST-COURSE SERVINGS

One 1-foot-long, 2-inch-thick precooked duck sausage (see page 107)
1 recipe brioche dough (see page 112)
Butter, for greasing pan
¼ cup heavy cream (optional)

TO SERVE
Dijon or whole-grain mustard (optional)
Cornichons (French sour gherkins; optional)

Place the sausage in a wide pot and cover by at least 2 inches with cold water. Bring to a gentle simmer and poach for 45 minutes. Transfer the sausage to a sheet pan and let cool until it's warm, not hot or cold. Gently peel off and discard the casing, handling the sausage gently so it doesn't break.

Reheat the sausage filling for a few minutes if necessary—it should be slightly warm. Use a floured rolling pin to shape the brioche dough into a 12-by-18-inch rectangle that's ½ inch thick. Don't worry if the corners of the rectangle are rounded. Arrange the sausage in a column down the center of the dough. Lift up the short edges of the dough and press them together to form a seam along the entire length of the sausage; seal

the ends, too. Place the whole assembly, seam side down, in a buttered loaf pan—mine is 13 by 4 by 4 inches.

Preheat the oven to 350°F. Cover the loaf with a sheet of plastic wrap and allow it to rise slightly, at room temperature, for 30 minutes. Remove the plastic wrap, brush the loaf with the heavy cream, if desired, and using a sharp knife, make a ⅓-inch-deep slit along the length of the bread to prevent it from cracking. Bake for 40 minutes until golden brown, or until the bread sounds hollow when tapped. Unmold onto a wire rack and cool for 5 minutes before cutting into slices with a bread knife to serve. I like to pass mustard and some cornichons.

Brioche

FOR THE SPONGE STARTER

⅓ cup warm milk (it should feel barely warm
    when you touch it with the back of a finger)
1 packet (2¼ teaspoons) active dried yeast
1 large egg
2 cups unbleached all-purpose flour

FOR THE DOUGH

⅓ cup sugar
1 teaspoon salt
4 large eggs, lightly beaten
1½ cups unbleached all-purpose flour, or more as needed
1½ sticks (12 tablespoons) unsalted butter, cut into
    ½-inch cubes and warmed to room temperature,
    plus 1 tablespoon unsalted butter, for greasing
    the bowl

To make the sponge: Place the milk, yeast, egg, and 1 cup of the flour in a mixing bowl or in the bowl of a heavy-duty electric mixer. Use a wooden spoon or the paddle blade to lightly combine these ingredients—there's no need for actual kneading at this point—and then sprinkle the remaining 1 cup flour over the surface of the mixture. (This prevents a crust from forming.) Let rest for 1 hour in a warm place. The flour will appear cracked on top when the sponge is ready.

To make the dough: Add the sugar, salt, eggs, and 1 cup of the flour to the sponge. Replace the paddle blade with the dough hook and work the mixture on slow speed until it just starts to pull together, about 2 minutes. If you're kneading by hand, work the mixture for about 2 minutes. Add another ½ cup of the flour and work the mixture on medium speed or by hand for 15 minutes. If you're using an electric mixer, periodically scrape down the sides of the bowl so everything gets incorporated. If, after 10 minutes, the dough seems loose, work in 1 to 3 tablespoons more flour until the dough holds together in a single mass. At this point it may cling to the sides of the bowl (or to your fingers), but it shouldn't leave behind any dough.

With the mixer on medium, add one-third of the softened butter and continue to work the dough for 5 minutes. Repeat with half of the remaining butter,

work for 5 minutes more, then add the rest of the butter. When the last of the butter is incorporated, work the mixture for 1 minute on high speed and 5 minutes more on medium, scraping down the sides of the bowl and the hook so everything gets evenly mixed in. If the dough seems loose after 2 minutes, add up to 2 tablespoons more flour. Don't be tempted to add more. The looseness just means that the butter has melted or softened, giving the impression that the brioche is too wet. If you're working by hand, knead the brioche with the heels of your hands on a flat surface, working in the butter and if necessary, additional flour, as described above.

Grease a large mixing bowl with the 1 tablespoon butter, then transfer the dough to it and cover with plastic wrap, with the plastic actually touching the sponge's surface so a crust doesn't form. Don't cover the sponge in such a way that it can't expand as it ferments. Let it rise in a warm place for 4 hours or until it's doubled in volume. Press down the dough so it compacts to its original volume and, cover the dough with plastic wrap as before, and refrigerate 6 hours or overnight. The dough may rise but not as much as it did in a warm place. After the cold rise, the deflated dough can be wrapped tightly in plastic wrap and frozen for up to 1 month. Thaw overnight in the refrigerator before using.

Duck Salami

In brief, a salami is a sausage that's been hung to dry and develop flavor. Theoretically at least, you could just hang your sausages in a cool place for 3 months and end up with salami. I, however, have played it safe and followed the advice in a recipe that came with my sausage maker to use something called "Prague powder," essentially a mixture of salt and potassium nitrate or potassium nitrite that the French call *sel rose*. I used to think that I could leave this out, assuming wrongly that the only function of potassium nitrite was to keep the salami pink instead of gray. But potassium nitrite turns to potassium nitrate as the meat ages, releasing nitric oxide in the process, a gas that kills microorganisms, making your salamis and other cured meats less likely to turn rancid. There is some controversy about sodium nitrate and nitrite forming carcinogenic compounds when cooked, but the research I've read suggests that this is primarily a problem with bacon and not with other meats. If you are concerned, you can leave it out; just know that your salami won't keep as long. I like serving homemade salami on a mixed duck hors d'oeuvre platter, along with duck prosciutto and rillettes.

MAKES FOUR 10- TO 12-INCH-LONG, 2-INCH-THICK SALAMIS

4 pounds duck meat taken from the legs or breasts (about 14 legs if
  you're using legs alone; about 18 breasts if using breasts alone)
1¼ pounds fatback, rind removed, cut into ½-inch cubes (1½ cups) and frozen
1 cup ice water
2½ tablespoons noniodized salt, or more as needed
1 teaspoon Prague powder No. 2 (see page 114)
2 tablespoons corn syrup solids (optional; see page 114)
1½ tablespoons freshly ground black pepper
2 tablespoons peppercorns, crushed under a heavy saucepan
1½ tablespoons powdered dextrose (see page 114)
1 cup soy protein concentrate (see page 114)
2 large cloves garlic, chopped fine and crushed to a paste with
  the side of a chefs' knife
½ teaspoon ground ginger
1 tablespoon olive oil
3½ feet of beef middle casings, rinsed and desalted
  as described on pages 104 to 105

Make sure that the duck and fatback are well chilled before you prepare the stuffing: Place all the ingredients except the olive oil and the casings in a bowl set over another bowl of ice. If you're using a food processor, put the duck leg meat in the freezer for 30 minutes to 1 hour to lightly freeze it and make it easier to chop. If you're using a grinder or the sausage attachment to a mixer, don't worry about freezing the meat—it will be harder to grind.

If you're using a food processor, work in small batches, pulsing the mixture until the pieces of meat and fat are about the size of peas. If you're using a grinder or the sausage attachment of your mixer (see Note), work the salami mixture through the grinder or attachment using the medium-size die until the meat and fat are the size of peas. If there are only two dies, use the larger.

Now the meat must be cured. Transfer it to a large plastic or other nonreactive container and spread it out in a layer no thicker than 5 inches deep. Cover it with plastic wrap—make sure the plastic touches the surface of the mixture—and refrigerate for 3 days. Test the mixture by sautéeing a small patty in olive oil; if necessary, add more noniodized salt to taste.

Stuff the casings, tying them off every 10 to 12 inches (see page 105 for directions), until you've used all the mixture. Hang the salamis in a cool dry place for 3 months, after which time they should be covered with white mold. (Don't fret, this is a good thing.)

Since it's cured, there's no need to refrigerate salami, even once it has been cut. I serve it as an hors d'oeuvre with crackers or bread, sometimes along with cheese, proscuitto, or bresaola.

NOTE: The sausage attachment fits on the mixer and has a tube with a perforated metal plate on the end. A propeller-like blade rotates against the plate, cutting and forcing the mixture through the tube.

Additives for Curing

Unless you're making sausages and cooking them right away, ground meats, including duck, must be cured to prevent the growth of harmful bacteria while the meat is aging. Of all the recipes in this book, the salami recipe is the only one that requires these additives. All of these additives can be purchased from the source on page 154.

DEXTROSE: A sugar that's much less sweet than regular table sugar (sucrose), dextrose is sometimes added to salami mixtures as a nutrient for the beneficial bacteria that produce a well-made salami's distinctive tang.

CORN SYRUP SOLIDS: While not essential, these provide flavor and encourage the natural and beneficial fermentation that takes place as salami ages.

INSTACURE NO. 1: A basic mixture used for foods such as sausages that are going to be cooked rather than cured and aged.

PICKLING SPICE: A mixture of spices. Available from The Sausage Maker (see page 154) and some supermarkets.

PRAGUE POWDER NO. 2: A mixture of sodium nitrate and sodium nitrite. The sodium nitrate breaks down into sodium nitrite. During this process, it releases nitric oxide—a gas—that kills pathogenic bacteria. It's sometimes sold as Instacure No. 2.

SOY PROTEIN: This is sometimes added to meat mixtures to lighten their texture and help them retain moisture. When I'm making regular sausage, not salami, I use bread crumbs soaked in broth or milk instead.

Soups

A SOUP IS ALMOST THE SAME THING as a stew, except that it has a higher proportion of liquid to solid. That means you can convert duck soups to duck stews, and vice versa, just by increasing or decreasing the amount of liquid.

To make most duck soups, start by making a broth with the back, wings, and legs (see page 8). After about 3 hours, when the meat on the legs falls easily off the bone and the backs come apart when you poke at them with a fork, strain the broth. Gently remove the legs from the strainer and reserve. Throw out the cooked backs and wings. Pull the skin off the legs and discard it, then take the meat off the legs and add it to the strained broth. I either save the duck breasts for a different dish—remember, they freeze well—or I sauté them at the last minute and top the soup with the rare slices.

Most of the world's chicken soups and stews can be converted to duck soups. In the recipes that follow, the variations come from adding different ingredients at different stages. A typical variation might call for sweating aromatic vegetables such as carrots and onions in duck fat, adding liquid (duck broth and/or wine), simmering duck thighs in the soup until the meat is falling off the bone, pulling away the meat, reuniting it with the soup, and discarding the bones. Flavorful elements such as herbs and garlic can be stirred in at the end, and various ingredients, such as rice, pasta, and vegetables, added at different stages, depending on their cooking times.

PREVIOUS PAGE: *A bowl of Duck, Cabbage, and Borlotti Bean* Potée. (recipe opposite).

Duck, Cabbage, and Borlotti Bean *Potée*

A potée is an archetypally French dish—half stew, half soup—made by simmering pork with vegetables, one of which is almost always cabbage. Duck takes especially well to the *potée* treatment, its rich savor balancing the leanness of the vegetables. I make *potées* with duck legs, saving the breasts for dishes that require less cooking. This version is very thick—almost like a cassoulet—so if you want it more souplike, just add a little more broth. The recipe makes a lot, but remember the *potée* will keep for 5 days in the refrigerator—or even longer if you bring it to a boil every 5 days—and for months in the freezer.

MAKES 12 MAIN-COURSE SERVINGS

2 cups dried borlotti, cannellini, or great Northern beans
12 uncooked duck legs or confit duck legs (see page 76)
Salt and pepper
¼ cup rendered duck fat (see page 8) or olive oil
2 medium carrots, peeled and sliced
2 medium onions, peeled, halved, and sliced as thin as possible
7 cloves garlic, peeled and chopped coarse
4 quarts brown duck broth (see page 8), chicken broth
(see page 10), or water, or more as needed
1 medium cabbage, preferably savoy or red cabbage, cored and sliced thin

Soak the beans in at least 6 quarts of water for 8 to 12 hours, and then drain them.

If you're using uncooked duck legs, season them with salt and pepper, and place them, skin side up, in a roasting pan or sheet pan just large enough to hold them in a single layer, so the fat doesn't run off and burn. Roast them for 2 hours in a 350°F oven.

An hour before the duck legs are done, heat the duck fat over medium heat in a pot large enough to hold the *potée;* add the carrots, onions, and garlic; and cook them until the onions turn translucent, about 15 minutes. Add the broth and the drained beans to the pot and simmer, covered, until the beans are soft, about 1½ hours. Check every 20 minutes—if the mixture starts to run dry, add more broth or water.

After 1 hour of simmering the beans, add the cabbage and the cooked duck legs—leave the rendered fat in the pan—or confit duck legs, and simmer, covered, for 30 minutes more. Season to taste with salt and pepper. Serve each guest a mound of vegetables—the *potée* will be more solid than liquid—with a duck leg on top.

Duck *Pho*

*T*he Vietnamese soup *pho*—pronounced like "foot" without the t—is as much a ritual as it is a meal. In most versions, a broth is made and seasoned, usually with cloves, cinnamon, star anise, and ginger, then various condiments are added to the soup before serving, or they are passed at the table for guests to help themselves. Since *pho* means "noodle," by definition the soup must always contain them, but the rest of the ingredients are limited only by your imagination and what you can find at the greengrocer or in the fridge. Some herbs, such as basil (preferably the small-leaf holy basil found in Asian markets), cilantro, and mint, add a lot of flavor to soups, used separately or in combination. A few chiles, added to provide heat, almost always make a worthwhile contribution. I sauté the duck breasts at the last minute, leaving them rare, then slice and arrange them on top of the noodles just before serving the soup. You can pass them at the table if you prefer.

There's nothing tricky about making a duck *pho*: The broth is the time-consuming part of this soup, but it can be made ahead of time and refrigerated for 5 days or frozen for months. To make the *pho* even more special, make a double-duck broth by using chicken or duck broth instead of water to simmer the duck parts.

MAKES 4 GENEROUS MAIN-COURSE OR 8 FIRST-COURSE SERVINGS

FOR THE BROTH
2 Pekin (Long Island) ducks (about 5 pounds each),
*   cut up as shown on pages 5 to 6*
Salt and pepper
3 tablespoons peanut oil or vegetable oil
1 medium onion, peeled and quartered
1 medium carrot, peeled and sliced
3 cloves garlic, peeled and crushed
4 quarts brown duck broth (see page 8), chicken broth
*   (see page 10), or water*
Four ¼-inch-thick slices fresh ginger
1 cinnamon stick, crushed under a pot
2 whole cloves
4 star anise (available at Asian groceries), crushed

FOR THE NOODLES
½ pound dried rice vermicelli noodles, soaked for 30 minutes
*   in warm water and drained*

FOR THE CONDIMENTS *(adjust quantities if you choose not to use them all)*
1 bunch cilantro, leaves only
1 bunch mint, leaves only
1 bunch basil, preferably a small-leaf variety such as holy basil
*   or Italian basilico piccolo, leaves only*
6 small chiles, such as Thai, jalapeño, or serrano, stemmed,
*   seeded, and chopped fine*
1 cup bean sprouts
1 cup fresh pineapple cubes (about ½ inch square)
4 ripe tomatoes, peeled, seeded, and chopped coarse
Thai fish sauce
Salt and pepper

Using a meat cleaver or heavy chefs' knife, break the duck backs into four pieces each and cut the wings, at the joints, into three pieces. Leave the skin on the legs. Score the skin on the breasts as shown on page 14.

Season the duck legs on both sides with salt and pepper and put them in a heavy-bottomed pot large enough to hold the soup, along with the oil. Cook them over medium to high heat until brown, about 5 minutes on each side. Take the legs out with tongs and put in the onion, carrot, garlic, and the cut-up duck backs and wings. Cook over medium to high heat, stirring every few minutes, for about 20 minutes, until the duck and vegetables are well browned, but not long enough to burn the bottom of the pot. Put the legs back in the pot and add the broth or water. Add the ginger, cinnamon, cloves, and star anise and bring to a simmer. Turn down the heat so the broth simmers gently and cook for 3 hours, skimming off the fat and froth that float to the top during simmering. Strain, preferably through a fine-mesh strainer. Remove the skin from the duck legs and discard it. Pull the meat away in shreds and add it to the strained broth.

Shortly before you're ready to serve, sauté the duck breasts as described on page 14 and arrange the condiments in your prettiest bowls—I put the fish sauce in a little vinegar pitcher. If you've let the duck broth cool, reheat it. Put about 1 cup of the strained duck broth in a saucepan big enough to hold the noodles, add the noodles, cover the pot, and put it on medium heat for about 2 minutes, until the noodles are completely soft—just grab one and taste it.

Arrange the noodles in mounds in heated soup bowls. If you're serving the soup with the breasts in it, slice them and arrange the slices in each bowl on top of the noodles. Keep the slices above the broth so they don't overcook and turn gray. Otherwise, put the sliced breasts on a plate for passing at the table. Ladle the broth around the noodles and serve immediately. Pass the condiments, including the fish sauce, at the table.

Chinese Hot-and-Sour Soup with Duck

I had tasted many restaurant versions of hot-and-sour soup, but it wasn't until I tried Barbara Tropp's recipe from *The Modern Art of Chinese Cooking* that I realized what I had been missing. She calls for only the best ingredients—and doesn't use too much cornstarch. Here I've adapted her recipe for duck, making a broth with the duck backs then braising the legs in the broth. If you like, sauté the duck breasts, slice them thin, and add them to the soup just before serving.

I've included most of the usual hot-and-sour soup ingredients—tiger lily stems, dried tree ears, and shiitake mushrooms—but only the shiitake mushrooms are essential. The caps of the best dried shiitakes are covered with fissures; less expensive and less flavorful, but still acceptable, are dried shiitakes with smooth caps or fresh shiitakes. When done the long way, this soup takes time, so I never bother making fewer than eight portions. Much of this soup can be prepared ahead of time, but the pepper must be added at the last minute or its aroma will cook off.

MAKES 8 FIRST-COURSE SERVINGS

1 Pekin (Long Island) duck (about 5 pounds)
1 medium onion, peeled and quartered
1 carrot, peeled and cut into ½-inch-thick slices
1 bouquet garni (5 sprigs fresh thyme or 1 teaspoon dried,
  1 imported bay leaf, and the stems from 1 bunch parsley,
  tied together with kitchen twine or wrapped in cheesecloth)
2 quarts chicken broth (see page 10) or water, plus more as needed
8 large or 16 small dried or fresh shiitake mushrooms, preferably Chinese
½ cup dried tree ears, soaked for 30 minutes in boiling water,
  drained, and rinsed (optional)
30 dried tiger lily stems (available in Asian groceries),
  soaked for 30 minutes in warm water (optional)
1 tablespoon cornstarch
½ cup sherry vinegar, balsamic vinegar, or excellent red wine vinegar,
  plus more to taste
1 or 2 small cakes (about 8 ounces total) soft tofu,
  cut into ½-inch cubes (optional)
3 tablespoons dark soy sauce, preferably a Japanese brand,
  plus more as needed
1 teaspoon dark sesame oil, preferably a Japanese brand
5 scallions, including the greens, sliced fine
1 tablespoon freshly ground black pepper
1 egg, beaten (optional)

Cut up the duck as shown on pages 5 to 6, breaking up the carcass and wings with a cleaver. Score the skin side of the breasts (see page 14), put them in a heavy-bottomed pot large enough to hold the soup, and sauté them, skin side down, over medium to high heat for about 7 minutes. Thinly slice the breasts and reserve them on a plate, covered with plastic wrap. Using the fat rendered from the breasts, brown the legs, starting skin side down, in the same pan, about 7 minutes for each side. When you remove the legs, replace them with the broken-up carcass and the onion and carrot. Brown these for about 10 minutes. Put the legs back in the pot with the bouquet garni, pour the broth or water, and bring to a gentle simmer. Simmer for 2 hours, covered, using a ladle to skim off fat and froth that float to the top.

While the duck broth is simmering, soak the dried shiitakes in just enough hot water to cover. If you're using fresh shiitakes, just cut off their stems and—only if the caps are large—cut them into quarters. When the dried mushrooms are soft and pliable, cut off their stems and—again, only if they're large—quarter the caps. Put the stems in the broth. Pull any hard pieces off the tree ears and discard them. If they seem too large to eat, tear them in half. Reserve the shiitake and tree ear caps. Pull the tiger lily stems into strands and reserve.

Gently remove the legs, then pull off the skin and tear away the meat in bite-size shreds, discarding the skin and reserving the meat. Strain the duck broth through a fine-mesh sieve into a clean pot, discarding the pieces of carcass and cooked vegetables, and skim off any fat with a ladle. Bring to a gentle simmer again. Mix the cornstarch with the vinegar and whisk into the simmering soup. Add the shiitakes, tree ears, tiger lily stems, tofu, soy sauce, sesame oil, scallions, reserved shredded duck leg and sliced breast, and the pepper. Taste the broth; if it needs more salt, add soy sauce; if it needs more tang, add vinegar.

Lower the heat and pour the beaten egg in a thin stream into the barely simmering soup. Stir gently, then continue cooking for a minute until the egg sets into thin strands. Ladle the soup into heated bowls and serve.

Chinese Duck and Noodle Soup

𝒪ne of the great things about Asian soups, especially Chinese soups, is the ease with which a little broth and seasoning can be turned into a complete meal, just by adding noodles. This is such a soup, inspired in part by soups I've eaten in Asian noodle shops and in part by its well-loved American cousin, chicken noodle soup. My knowledge of Chinese cooking is skimpy, but with a few Chinese ingredients, I'm able to make a Chinese-seeming soup out of just about anything. The secret ingredients are ginger, garlic, soy sauce (I prefer Japanese brands), scallions, and dark Asian sesame oil (again, Japanese brands are best). Dried shiitake mushrooms contribute a deep, meaty flavor, as well as contrasting texture to this soup. The time-consuming part of this dish, cooking the duck legs, can be done up to 3 days ahead of time, or even longer if you freeze the legs and the broth. This soup is a great way to use duck legs you've saved up in the freezer.

MAKES 6 FIRST-COURSE OR LIGHT MAIN-COURSE SERVINGS

3 tablespoons vegetable oil
6 duck legs
2 quarts cold brown duck broth (see page 8), chicken broth
   (see page 10), or water
1 pound fresh Chinese egg noodles, fettuccine, or linguini
2 tablespoons freshly grated ginger (see Note)
3 cloves garlic, peeled, chopped fine, and crushed to a paste
   with the side of a chefs' knife
4 tablespoons dark soy sauce, preferably a Japanese brand,
   plus more to taste
2 teaspoons dark sesame oil, preferably a Japanese brand
5 scallions, including the greens, sliced thin
Freshly ground black pepper

Heat 2 tablespoons of the vegetable oil in a heavy-bottomed sauté pan, add the duck legs, and sauté over medium heat to high heat for about 8 minutes on each side, until well browned. Put the legs in a pot big enough to hold the soup and pour in the cold broth or water. Bring to a gentle simmer and continue simmering for about 1½ hours, using a ladle to skim off fat and froth that float to the top.

In another pot, bring about 4 quarts water, with the remaining 1 tablespoon vegetable oil, to a boil, add the noodles, and boil until they're al dente—when you bite into a piece, it offers a little resistance, but it's in no way raw.

While the noodles are cooking, stir the ginger, garlic, soy sauce, sesame oil, and scallions into the gently simmering broth and simmer for about 2 minutes to cook the scallions.

When the noodles are ready, drain them in a colander, then divide them among heated deep Asian-style bowls. Use a skimmer to place a duck leg on top of each mound of noodles. Taste the broth and adjust the sea-sonings; if it seems to need salt, add more soy sauce instead. Add freshly ground pepper to taste. Ladle the broth over the noodles and duck legs, and serve.

NOTE: For ginger that's almost puréed, cut the peel off a 2-inch length of the root and grate it on the finest grater you have.

Duck Wonton Soup

It may sound like a peculiar combination of French and Chinese cuisines, but duck rillettes (shredded duck confit preserved with a thin layer of duck fat) can be used as a wonton filling. When the wontons are heated, the duck fat melts so that as you bite into each wonton, it bursts with flavor. To accentuate the drama, I serve the wontons surrounded by an understated broth and give my guests only spoons so they don't cut into the wontons with a knife or fork and spoil the effect. The rillettes filling follows my standard recipe, except that I've replaced the French spices with typically Chinese seasonings—ginger, garlic, soy sauce, and dark sesame oil.

MAKES 6 FIRST-COURSE SERVINGS (42 WONTONS)

1½ cups duck rillettes (see page 83), minus the spices
1 tablespoon grated fresh ginger
1 clove garlic, peeled, chopped fine, and crushed to a paste
 with the side of a chefs' knife
1 tablespoon soy sauce
2 teaspoons dark sesame oil, preferably a Japanese brand
3 scallions, half the green parts discarded, chopped fine,
 plus 1 whole scallion, sliced fine
Salt
42 square wonton wrappers (usually about 60 come in each package)
6 cups chicken broth (see page 10)

Combine the rillettes, ginger, garlic, soy sauce, sesame oil, and chopped scallions in a mixing bowl. Season to taste with salt.

Assemble the wontons one at a time. Brush one side of the wrapper with water to make it pliable and place a mounded teaspoon of the rillette filling in its center. Bring one corner to meet the opposite corner and pinch along both edges to seal. Brush one of the two remaining corners with water and bring these two together, pinching them to seal. When all the wontons are filled and shaped, give them a final pinch; you should end up with rings that are thin on one side and thick—full of filling—on the other. Transfer them to a sheet pan lined with wax paper—don't stack them or they might stick together—cover with plastic wrap, and refrigerate or freeze until needed (see Note).

Bring the chicken broth to a simmer in a large pot and add the wontons. Cook them gently for 5 minutes—don't boil them or they might burst open. Add the sliced scallion, and continue simmering for 1 minute more. Spoon the broth into heated soup bowls and add seven wontons to each bowl.

NOTE: To make and freeze the wontons ahead of time, lightly dust a sheet pan with flour, arrange the wontons on top so that they don't touch each other, and slide the pan into the freezer. When the wontons have frozen, after 40 minutes or so, immediately transfer them to plastic bags and return them to the freezer. This method prevents the wontons from clumping together.

Duck Bouillabaisse

𝒞alling this soup a bouillabaisse is a stretch, since not a piece of fish comes near it. But the Mediterranean flavors of a traditional bouillabaisse—the garlic, tomatoes, and saffron—are a perfect match for duck legs. If you're using duck confit, you'll need to use chicken broth or to make duck broth from the backs and wings, but in a pinch you can get by using water because the tomatoes and garlic are so flavorful.

This soup has several different elements: tomato broth, roasted garlic purée, basil puréed with cream, and saffron soaked in a small amount of water. Most recipes would combine each of these elements into one soup with homogeneous flavors. As an alternative, I deconstructed this soup, leaving these elements separate, then swirling or sprinkling them over the soup at serving time so the dish becomes a study in contrasts.

MAKES 8 LIGHT MAIN-COURSE SERVINGS OR SUBSTANTIAL FIRST-COURSE SERVINGS

8 duck legs, including both thighs and drumsticks
Salt and pepper
5 tablespoons rendered duck fat (see page 15) or olive oil
1 large onion, peeled and chopped
6 ripe tomatoes, chopped coarse (don't bother peeling or seeding them)
1 cup white wine
2 quarts brown duck broth (see page 8), chicken broth
    (see page 10), or water
1 bouquet garni (6 sprigs thyme, 1 bunch parsley, and
    1 imported bay leaf, tied together with kitchen twine)
4 heads garlic, broken up into cloves but not peeled
½ cup heavy cream
1 bunch basil, leaves only (about ⅔ cup tightly packed)
8 slices crusty French bread, about ½ inch thick, toasted
½ teaspoon saffron threads, soaked for 30 minutes
    in 2 tablespoons hot water

Season the duck legs with salt and pepper. Heat 3 tablespoons of the duck fat in a heavy-bottomed pot large enough to hold the soup, and brown the legs over medium to high heat for about 5 minutes on each side. Take out the duck legs and cook the onion in the fat over medium heat for about 5 minutes. Put the legs back in the pot, add the tomatoes, wine, and just enough of the broth or water to cover. Nestle in the bouquet garni. Bring to a simmer, then turn down the heat to maintain the simmer for 1 hour, using a ladle to skim off the fat and froth that float to the top.

Coat the garlic cloves with the remaining 2 tablespoons duck fat and wrap them together in a sheet of aluminum foil. Put them in the oven, set the temperature to 400°F—there's no need for preheating—and roast them for about 45 minutes, until the cloves feel completely soft when you squeeze them through the aluminum foil. Transfer the unpeeled garlic to a blender, add 2 cups cooking liquid from the duck legs, and purée for about 1 minute, starting with short pulses to keep the hot mixture from shooting out the top. Work this garlic mixture through a food mill, or use a ladle to push it through a fine-mesh strainer, and reserve the garlic broth in a small bowl.

When you're almost ready to serve the soup, heat the cream in a small saucepan until hot but not boiling. (This is to keep it from turning into butter when you work it in the blender.) Combine the basil leaves with the hot cream in the blender—firmly hold the top on the blender with a towel so the liquid doesn't shoot out—and purée for about 30 seconds, starting with very short pulses with the blender set to its lowest setting. Transfer the basil mixture to a small bowl, cover with plastic wrap—the wrap should touch the surface of the puree to keep the basil from turning dark—and reserve. Take the legs out of the tomato broth and work the broth through a food mill or fine-mesh strainer—discarding the bouquet garni—and put the broth back in the pot. Bring it to a simmer and season to taste with salt and pepper, then put the legs back in the soup to reheat them. Heat the garlic broth in the microwave or in a saucepan.

Place a piece of toast in the center of each heated soup bowl and place a duck leg on top. Spoon over the tomato broth, swirl over the garlic broth, add the basil mixture in Jackson Pollock–like streaks, and place the saffron threads with their soaking liquid here and there over the duck legs. Serve the bouillabaisse immediately, providing a knife, fork, and spoon for each guest.

Duck Breasts with Smoke-Scented Broth

*M*any of us don't like to serve food with rich sauces but still want to accent or extend the flavors of whatever dish we're cooking. Serving meat (or fish) with a savory broth provides a lighter alternative to a concentrated sauce while still contributing plenty of flavor. The obvious choice here is duck broth, made from the duck's back and legs and perhaps flavored with fresh herbs, mushrooms (wild or otherwise), bits of bacon, and baby vegetables (or larger vegetables cut into small shapes). Even more dramatic is broth with a smoky flavor, which you can make a couple of ways. You can infuse duck broth with smoked ingredients—again, bacon comes in handy; you can make a duck broth from grilled duck legs; or you can use dashi, a Japanese broth made from flakes of smoked bonito, a fish related to tuna. If the idea of coupling fish with meat sounds too weird, don't fret. Dashi imparts a subtle smokiness to most foods and tastes very little like fish.

When serving duck breasts with hot savory broth, you have to be careful that the duck doesn't poach in the hot broth and overcook. To avoid this, prop the sliced duck breast on top of the vegetables, out of the broth's reach. Here I call for watercress flavored with sesame oil, but any leafy vegetable will do.

MAKES 4 MAIN-COURSE SERVINGS

4 Pekin (Long Island) duck breasts or 2 mullard breasts
    (1½ to 2 pounds total)
Salt and pepper
1 long strip konbu seaweed (4 by 18 inches or the equivalent)
4 cups cold brown duck broth (see page 8), chicken broth
    (see page 10), or water
One 1-ounce bag bonito flakes (about 3½ cups if not packed down)
2 bunches watercress
1 teaspoon dark sesame oil, preferably a Japanese brand

Using a long, thin, very sharp knife, score the skin of the duck breasts about 20 times in two directions (see page 14 for more detailed instructions). Season the breasts on both sides with salt and pepper, cover with plastic wrap, and refrigerate. An hour before serving time, take the duck breasts out of the refrigerator so they warm to room temperature. If you cook them cold, they'll be overcooked on the outside and raw in the middle.

Break the konbu into a couple of pieces and put it in a saucepan with the cold broth or water. Bring the broth to a simmer, adjusting the heat so this takes about 15 minutes, then remove the cooked konbu—it should be bright green now—with a pair of tongs and discard it. (Some cooks reuse konbu, but I don't bother.) Pour the bonito flakes into the hot, konbu-flavored broth and let them sit for 1 minute, then strain the dashi into a clean saucepan—discarding the bonito flakes—and reserve.

In another saucepan, bring about 2 quarts water with 2 tablespoons salt to a rapid boil. Cut off and discard the thicker stems of the watercress, but don't bother taking the leaves off the very small stems. Plunge the watercress into the boiling water and boil for 30 seconds to eliminate the bitterness. Drain in a colander, rinse under cold running water, and squeeze out excess water with your hands. Reserve the watercress in the saucepan.

Sauté or grill the duck breasts according to the directions on page 14. Add 1 tablespoon water and the sesame oil to the watercress, and place the saucepan over low heat. When the watercress is hot, season it to taste with salt, tossing to combine. Place small mounds of watercress in heated soup bowls, then slice the duck breasts and arrange the slices on top of the watercress. Spoon the hot dashi around the duck—not over it, or you'll turn the slices gray—and serve.

Dashi

There are several ways to make dashi, none of which requires much effort beyond a trip to an Asian grocery store. First you can buy instant dashi and just follow the instructions on the package. I don't recommend this, since it's loaded with MSG, but instant dashi is useful stuff to have on hand for last-minute emergencies. A more traditional approach is to buy shredded bonito flakes—they're easy to spot since they look like wood shavings—and infuse them for 1 minute in water that's been brought to a boil and then removed from heat. If you're interested in age-old methods, you can shave the dried bonito yourself—it looks like an overripe banana but it's hard like wood—using a special device that looks like a cross between a wood plane and a shoe box. I opt for buying the bonito flakes already shaved: Whole dried bonito is hard to find, and the shaving gadget is expensive for something that has only one use.

Once you have the bonito, you'll need seaweed. Go to a Japanese market, where they offer a baffling assortment of seaweeds, each with a particular flavor and texture. You'll be looking for konbu (or kombu), a very dark green, almost black seaweed that comes in strips 2 to 4 inches wide and about 18 inches long. It will be lightly dusted with white salt-like minerals, a natural coating that delivers a lot of flavor.

Salads

DUCK IS SO SAVORY that it makes a marvelous addition to a green salad. A salad also offers a good way of using duck legs; sliced thin and served on top of fresh greens, they don't give the impression of toughness, as duck legs sometimes do if served whole on a plate. One of my favorite summer salads is a mixture of basil and arugula leaves tossed at the last minute with vinaigrette and sliced grilled or sautéed duck breasts or slow-roasted duck legs. In the winter I use endive.

Endive and Duck Confit Salad

*C*ool and crunchy, bitter and sweet, endive cut into little strips partners beautifully with shreds of duck confit. I sneak in a tiny bit of orange zest, since orange goes great with both confit and endive. Nuts, pecans or walnuts, add contrasting texture. Nuts of course bring to mind the idea of using nut oils in the vinaigrette, but beware—nut oils turn rancid so quickly that they're sometimes even bad by the time you first open the bottle (see Nut Oils, page 135). The sauce for this salad contains a little heavy cream, which will emulsify the nut oil with the vinegar. In most vinaigrettes, this is accomplished with mustard, but mustard interferes with the flavor of the nut oil. The dressing for this salad can be made ahead of time. If you julienne the endive more than an hour in advance, keep it in a bowl of cold water to prevent it from wilting.

MAKES 4 FIRST-COURSE SERVINGS

1 orange
2 tablespoons heavy cream
2 tablespoons sherry vinegar
4 tablespoons walnut, hazelnut, or pistachio oil (see Nut Oils,
   page 135), or extra-virgin olive oil
Salt and pepper
2 confit duck legs, smoked if desired (see pages 76 and 92)
3 heads Belgian endive
½ cup pecans or walnut halves, toasted for 15 minutes in a 300°F oven
¼ cup parsley leaves, chopped fine at the very last minute

Use a sharp paring knife to cut a 2-inch strip of zest off the orange—shave off any pith that may remain attached to the inside of the strip—and cut the zest into very fine julienne, or chop it fine. Combine the zest with the heavy cream and the vinegar in a bowl big enough to toss the salad, and gently whisk in the oil, about ½ teaspoon at a time. Season to taste with salt and pepper, but go easy on the salt, since the confit is already salty.

Take the skin off the confit and discard it. Pull away the meat in shreds, but don't make them too fine. If you have trouble getting the meat off, heat the legs in a microwave for 30 seconds or wrap them in aluminum foil and heat in a 300°F oven for 15 minutes. Reserve.

Take the leaves off the endives (see How to Deal with Endive, below), then slice them in half lengthwise to make them easier to work with. Slice each of the halves into ¼-inch-wide strips. Wash in cold water—use a big bowl and lift the endive out with your fingers splayed—and spin or pat dry. Just before serving—in fact ideally at the table—toss the endive, confit, and nuts in the bowl with the dressing. Sprinkle each serving with the parsley.

Nut Oils

Frightfully perishable, nut oils can turn stale in a matter of weeks, even when tightly sealed and stored in the refrigerator. I use only one brand of nut oils, Leblanc (see Sources, page 154). Leblanc's oils are made from roasted nuts. The roasting brings out the flavor of the nuts and also destroys some of the compounds that cause rancidity. Leblanc makes walnut oil, hazelnut oil, and a magnificent (and expensive) green pistachio oil. I like the pistachio oil the best, partly because it has such an unusual flavor. Because it hasn't become common in restaurants, it catches your guests or family delightfully off guard.

How to Deal with Endive

As you pull away the individual leaves from the tight little bunch that is Belgian endive, the leaves get shorter. You can get them to come away all at once by slicing the base of the endive a couple inches from the bottom, but then you waste a lot. I start by slicing off the base of the endive about ½ inch from the bottom, and then I pull away as many leaves as I can without breaking them. Then I make another slice ½ inch above the first and pull away more leaves. I continue in this way until there's a tiny little piece in the middle that can be sliced but usually ends up popped into my mouth.

Wild Mushroom and Duck Confit Salad

*T*his salad is good when made with cultivated mushrooms like creminis, but with wild mushrooms, it enters the realm of the celestial.

MAKES 4 FIRST-COURSE OR LIGHT MAIN-COURSE SERVINGS

3 confit duck legs (see page 76)
¼ cup rendered duck fat (see page 15)
1 pound assorted wild mushrooms, such as porcini, morels,
    hedgehogs, and chanterelles, rinsed and patted dry
    (large mushrooms like porcini should be sliced)
¼ cup extra-virgin olive oil
¼ cup sherry vinegar, balsamic vinegar, or good-quality
    red wine vinegar, plus more as needed
Salt and pepper
4 large handfuls mixed or individual salad greens, such as arugula,
    curly endive, frisée, basil leaves, baby oak leaf lettuce, or
    baby hearts of romaine, washed and dried

Pull the skin off the duck legs, chop it into small pieces, and reserve. Pull the meat away from the bone in thin strips and reserve. Heat the duck fat in a large sauté pan over high heat, add the mushrooms, and sauté until they smell fragrant and any liquid they release has evaporated. Add the chopped duck skin, the shredded duck meat, olive oil, and vinegar to the still-hot pan, and toss or stir until well combined. Season to taste with salt and pepper. Put the salad greens in a large bowl, add the hot mushroom and duck mixture, and toss—I like to toss at the table just before serving. Taste a leaf, and if necessary, adjust the salt, pepper, or vinegar.

Duck Breast, Green Bean, and Artichoke Salad

Artichokes are a great foil for thin slices of sautéed duck breast, lightening the effect of the rich duck with their mild flavor and gentle texture. I add walnuts to take the study in contrasts a step farther. You can make this salad with artichoke hearts out of a jar, but because the brine in jarred artichokes is somewhat aggressive, I prefer fresh ones. There are three ways you can deal with fresh artichokes. You can cook the whole artichokes and serve them for dinner the night before, warning everyone that they can't eat the hearts; you can use baby artichokes, which have undeveloped chokes; or you can "turn" large artichokes, the classic French technique for eliminating all the leaves so you end up with only the hearts (see page 26).

MAKES 6 MAIN-COURSE SERVINGS

4 Pekin (Long Island) duck breasts or 2 mullard breasts,
    scored and sautéed as described on page 14
6 large artichokes or 18 baby artichokes, fresh or
    out of a jar (thoroughly rinse jarred artichokes)
2 tablespoons fresh lemon juice (unless you're using
    artichokes out of a jar)
6 tablespoons extra-virgin olive oil
½ pound green beans, preferably French-style haricots verts
Salt
1 cup walnut halves or pecans,
    toasted for 15 minutes in a 350°F oven
1 bunch curly endive (sometimes called chicory), frisée, or
    other crisp salad green, any wilted parts broken off,
    cut into large bite-size pieces, spun or patted dry
2 tablespoons sherry vinegar or good-quality red wine vinegar
Pepper
1 bunch fresh chervil, or 1 tablespoon chopped parsley

Allow the sautéed duck breasts to cool to room temperature. If you're working ahead of time, you can refrigerate them, well covered, for up to 3 days.

Prepare the artichoke bottoms as described above or in the box on page 26. If you're using raw artichokes, simmer the trimmed artichokes in salted water with 1 tablespoon of the olive oil (which prevents them from darkening) until they can be penetrated with a knife but offer some resistance, about 12 minutes for baby artichokes, 20 minutes for large artichoke bottoms. Cut the artichoke bottoms into six wedges. If you're using the baby artichokes, jarred or fresh, cut them in half vertically. Toss the fresh artichokes with the lemon juice and 1 tablespoon of the olive oil, or toss the jarred artichokes with the oil only. Reserve until needed, up to 24 hours in the refrigerator.

Cook the green beans in boiling salted water until they offer just a tiny bit of resistance when you bite into one, about 6 minutes. Drain, rinse with cold water, and spin or pat dry.

Put the beans, walnuts, artichokes, and endive in a large bowl. Toss with the remaining 4 tablespoons olive oil and the vinegar. Season to taste with salt and pepper and toss again.

Slice the duck breasts crosswise as thin as you can. Season the slices with salt and pepper. Place a mound of salad in the center of each plate and arrange the duck slices over the mounds. Decorate each salad with a sprig or two of chervil or a sprinkling of parsley, and serve.

Chinese Shredded Duck Salad

*I*first had a dish similar to this at a Chinese restaurant in Manhattan called Uncle Thai's. To this day, I still remember the food at that restaurant as the best Chinese food—even some of the best of any food—that I've ever tasted. Especially outstanding were the restaurant's shredded dishes, in which contrasts and savors worked their magic. Years later I read a recipe for a salad similar to one I had tasted at Uncle Thai's in Barbara Tropp's thorough and insightful *Modern Art of Chinese Cooking*. Here I suggest using a whole roast duck, but you can also use confit or meat from slow-roasted duck legs.

MAKES 6 FIRST-COURSE OR 4 LIGHT MAIN-COURSE SERVINGS

1 whole roast duck (see page 63), 4 confit duck legs (see page 76),
*   or 4 slow-roasted duck legs (see page 70)*
3 stalks celery
2 large carrots, peeled
½ pound snow peas, ends broken off and discarded
1 red bell pepper, stemmed and seeded

FOR THE SAUCE
2 cloves garlic, peeled, chopped fine, and crushed to a paste
*   with the side of a chefs' knife*
2 teaspoons dark sesame oil, preferably a Japanese brand
1 tablespoon honey
2 tablespoons soy sauce
3 tablespoons chopped cilantro leaves
1 tablespoon hoisin sauce (available in Asian groceries)
3 jalapeño chiles, stemmed, seeded, and chopped fine

Pull the skin off the duck and cut the meat into thin shreds no more than ⅛ inch thick and about 2 inches long. Pull the fat off the skin and shred the skin in the same way as the meat. Cut the celery into 2-inch sections and cut these lengthwise, also into ⅛-inch shreds. Cut the carrots into 2-inch sections and slice these lengthwise into ⅛-inch-thick strips. (A plastic vegetable slicer or mandoline comes in handy here.) Cut the carrot strips into shreds slightly smaller than ⅛ inch thick, cut the snow peas lengthwise into ⅛-inch shreds, and cut the bell pepper into ⅛-inch-thick strips. Combine all the shredded ingredients in a large nonreactive bowl and keep covered in the refrigerator for up to 1 day, until you're ready to serve.

Combine all the ingredients for the sauce in a small bowl and toss with the salad. Serve on individual plates or in bowls.

Terrines
and Mousses

A TERRINE IS A PÂTÉ that's baked in a loaf pan. We don't call it a pâté because purists insist that a genuine pâté is baked in a crust, a construction that is now redundantly called a pâté en croute. I never bother making pâté en croute—a terrine in a crust—because the surrounding dough absorbs the juices released during cooking, making the crust soggy and the meatless flavorful.

Most terrines are enriched with fatback—unsmoked pork belly—to keep them moist. Don't try leaving it out or cutting down on the amount or your terrine will be dry. Some terrines, such as the one on page 144, are held together with a clear concentrated broth that is allowed to set. These are usually called something like *terrine de canard* (duck) *en gelée*. A mousse differs from a terrine in that it is lighter—mousse means "foam" in French—and is made from very finely puréed duck meat or, even better, duck liver that's been lightened with butter and/or whipped cream.

The ultimate duck terrine is terrine of foie gras. Foie gras is the giant liver of an exercise-deprived duck that's been eating too much. Making a terrine out of these enormous livers isn't particularly difficult, but since store-bought terrines can be as good as homemade versions—and the ingredients for a whole terrine are frightfully expensive—I don't give a recipe here. When buying terrine of foie gras, look for the word *entier;* it means that the terrine was made from whole livers instead of liver purée. Terrines made from puréed livers are labeled "mousse" and should be less expensive. While foie gras mousse can be every bit as flavorful as terrines made from the whole livers, the firm, butterlike texture of the whole livers is missing.

LEFT: *A slice of duck terrine with crusty bread.*

Duck Terrine

*T*he simplest terrines are made by grinding all the ingredients together in a food processor or meat grinder, packing the mixture into a fat-lined terrine, and baking it. The result is a kind of glorified meat loaf—not bad, but better things are possible. In this duck terrine, a fine forcemeat—a purée of meat, fat, and chicken livers—provides a smooth texture and deep meaty flavor, keeps the terrine moist, and binds it together. Coarsely chopped duck meat and prosciutto contribute texture and bright bits of flavor. Cubes of duck breast, fatback, and bright green pistachios vary the flavor and provide color and contrasting textures. Bread crumbs combined with milk are added to give the terrine a lighter texture.

MAKES ONE 2-LITER TERRINE (MINE MEASURES 11½ BY 4 BY 4 INCHES),
OR ABOUT 20 FIRST-COURSE SERVINGS

FOR THE GARNITURE

14 ounces fatback, rind removed, cut into ¼-inch dice
1 small clove garlic, peeled, chopped fine, and crushed to
    a paste with the side of a chefs' knife
2 tablespoons cognac
2 Pekin (Long Island) duck breasts, or 1 mullard breast,
    about 1 pound total, skin removed and discarded,
    meat cut into ¼-inch dice
¼ cup semi-dry Madeira or port (optional)

FOR THE FINE FORCEMEAT

¼ pound duck or chicken livers (about 3 whole livers), or a combination
6 ounces pork shoulder meat or one ¾-pound
    pork shoulder chop, boned, cut into 1-inch cubes
14 ounces fatback, rind removed, cut into ½-inch cubes
2 large eggs
2 large cloves garlic, peeled, chopped fine, and crushed to
    a paste with the side of a chefs' knife
1 teaspoon finely chopped fresh thyme or ½ teaspoon dried
2 teaspoons freshly ground black pepper
½ teaspoon ground cloves
½ teaspoon ground ginger
¼ teaspoon ground nutmeg
4 slices dense-crumb white bread, crusts removed
⅔ cup brown duck broth (see page 8), or chicken broth
    (see page 10), or milk

FOR THE COARSE FORCEMEAT
2 duck legs
6 ounces prosciutto (pork, not duck)
½ cup (2 ounces) shelled pistachios
1 teaspoon finely chopped fresh marjoram (optional)

FOR TESTING, THEN ASSEMBLING THE TERRINE
1 tablespoon olive oil or rendered duck fat (see page 15),
*   or more as needed*
Salt and pepper
¾ pound fatback (not including the rind), sliced into thin sheets,
*   ½ pound caul fat, or ¼ pound thinly sliced bacon*

FOR SERVING (OPTIONAL)
Cornichons (French sour gherkins)
Dijon or whole-grain mustard

To prepare the garniture: Toss together all the garniture ingredients and marinate in the refrigerator for at least 2 hours or overnight.

To prepare the fine forcemeat: Combine the livers, pork shoulder, fatback, eggs, garlic, thyme, and spices in a food processor and purée the mixture until smooth, about 3 minutes, scraping down the inside walls of the processor every minute. Transfer the forcemeat to a mixing bowl. If the concentrated duck broth has set in the refrigerator, melt it on the stove. Use your fingers to break up and combine the bread slices with the broth or milk—don't overdo it or you'll make the mixture heavy—and then work the soaked bread into the rest of the forcemeat. Refrigerate until you're ready to assemble the terrine.

To prepare the coarse forcemeat: Peel the skin off the duck legs and discard it (or save it and render it for cooking). Cut the meat away from the bone and remove away any obvious strips of sinew, but don't get obsessive—a little bit is harmless. Coarsely chop the duck meat and the prosciutto, either by hand with a sharp chefs' knife or by chilling it in the freezer until it's almost frozen and then quickly pulsing it in a food processor, until the pieces are about the size of baby peas.

If the pistachios still have their thin peels, plunge them in boiling water for about 30 seconds, then rub them quickly in a kitchen towel to remove the peels. If the pistachios are large (as most are now since the little ones from Afghanistan are no longer imported), chop them coarse. If you're using the marjoram, use your fingers to combine it with the duck, prosciutto, and pistachios in a small mixing bowl and reserve the mixture until you're ready to assemble the terrine. If you're not using the marjoram, just stir the chopped duck, prosciutto, and pistachios into the fine forcemeat.

To test the filling: If you haven't done so, stir the coarse forcemeat into the fine forcemeat and work in the garniture. Stir any cognac, Madeira, or port used for marinating the garniture into the forcemeat. Form a walnut-size piece of the filling into a small patty and cook it like a hamburger in the olive oil. Taste, and adjust the salt and pepper accordingly. Test the mixture until it's seasoned the way you want it.

To fill the terrine: Line the 2-liter terrine with the fatback, caul, or bacon, leaving enough hanging over the sides to fold up and cover the top once you've filled the terrine. Fill the terrine with the duck mixture and tap the terrine a couple of times against a cutting board to help the mixture settle. Fold the fatback over the top. Cover the terrine with a triple sheet of aluminum foil folded at the corners as though making a bed.

To bake the terrine: Preheat the oven to 350°F. Put the terrine in a pan with sides at least 3 inches high. Bring a tea kettle of water to a boil. Place the terrine in its pan on a rack in the oven, and pour the boiling water into the pan until it comes halfway up the sides of the terrine. Bake the terrine until an instant-read thermometer stuck in the middle reads 145°F, about 90 minutes.

Remove the terrine from the hot-water bath, place a pan or cutting board on top of the terrine to weight it while it cools—so it doesn't crumble when you slice it—and let cool for 2 hours at room temperature, then overnight in the refrigerator. If you don't have something that fits directly on the surface of the terrine, fold over several layers of cardboard and place cans or a saucepan on top of that. If well sealed, the terrine will keep in the refrigerator for several weeks—in fact its flavor will improve.

When you're ready to serve, run a long thin knife around the sides of the terrine and turn it out onto a cutting board. If you've lined the terrine with caul fat, peel it off all at once and discard. If you've lined it with sheets of fatback or bacon, let each guest remove his or her own from each slice. Put a chilled slice on each plate—it's nice to serve the terrine at the table—and pass the cornichons and mustard, if desired.

Duck Terrine with Fresh Parsley

I admit that this terrine is labor-intensive, but you can start a day or two ahead of time and break the work up into stages. It is a derivative of a famous French dish, *jambon persillé,* in which ham is layered in a terrine with its congealed poaching liquid and plenty of chopped fresh parsley.

MAKES 15 FIRST-COURSE SERVINGS (USE A 2-LITER TERRINE—
MINE MEASURES 11½ BY 4 BY 4 INCHES)

2 Pekin (Long Island) ducks (about 10 pounds total)
3 onions, peeled and quartered
3 medium carrots, peeled and cut into 1-inch pieces
4 quarts chicken broth (see page 10) or water (optional)
2 bouquets garnis (each containing 5 sprigs fresh thyme or
*   1 teaspoon dried, 2 imported bay leaves, and 1 bunch parsley,*
*   tied together with kitchen string or wrapped in cheesecloth)*
3 tablespoons olive oil or rendered duck fat (see page 15)
4 ripe tomatoes, peeled, seeded, and chopped coarse (see page 59)
2 cups red wine
1 package (¼ ounce) unflavored gelatin softened in
*   ½ cup warm water, if needed*
Salt and pepper
1 bunch flat-leaf parsley, chopped fine just before you use it

FOR SERVING (OPTIONAL)
Cornichons (French sour gherkins)
Pickled pearl onions
Dijon or whole-grain mustard

Cut up the ducks as described on pages 4 to 5. Save the fat in the freezer for making confit, and reserve the breasts and legs in the refrigerator. Cut the backs and the wings into three sections each with a heavy cleaver. Roast them in a roasting pan in an oven set at 425°F, with two of the onions and two of the carrots, for about 1 hour, until well browned. If the juices start to burn on the bottom of the pan, add about 1 quart chicken broth or water.

Transfer the duck backs and vegetables to a narrow pot—narrow makes it easier to skim—and deglaze the pan with 1 quart chicken broth or water (unless you added it earlier to prevent burning).

Put the deglazed juices in the pot with the backs. Add enough cold chicken broth or water to cover, put in one of the bouquets garnis, and bring to a simmer. Place the pot off-center over the flame so it simmers on one side only and use a ladle to skim off any fat or

froth that float to the top. Don't let the broth boil at any point or it will cloud and spoil the look of your terrine. Simmer for 3 hours and strain.

Brown the duck legs on both sides in the oil and put them in a narrow pot with the remaining onion, carrot, and bouquet garni. Pour in the duck broth, tomatoes, and red wine. Bring to a simmer and cook gently for 2 hours, skimming off the fat and froth the same way you did with the duck broth. Strain the broth and gently pull out the four duck legs. Let the duck legs cool, and strain the broth again through a fine-mesh sieve into a clean pot. Simmer gently, skimming again, until you have only 4 cups left, then remove from the heat.

At this point you must test the braising liquid to make sure that it sets firmly enough to hold the terrine together. Chill 1 cup of it in the refrigerator until it sets—this will happen faster if you put it in something wide—and you can judge its consistency. It should feel "bouncy" to the touch and not leave your finger wet. If it does, stir the gelatin mixture into the broth. (Put back the cup that you removed to test.)

Peel and cut the skin off the duck breasts. Season them with salt and pepper and sauté them for 2 to 4 minutes on each side, until they spring back to the touch. Reserve and let cool. Cut the breast meat into ⅓-inch cubes and keep covered with plastic wrap. Pull the skin off the duck legs—there's no need for cooking—and discard it. Pull the meat away from the bone in shreds. Cover with plastic wrap and reserve.

When you're ready to assemble the terrine, bring the duck braising liquid to a gentle simmer, stir in the parsley, and season to taste with salt and pepper, keeping in mind that it will taste less salty once cold. Arrange one-third of the shredded duck leg meat in the terrine and ladle 1 cup of the melted braising liquid over it. Chill in the refrigerator until set, about 30 minutes.

Arrange half the duck breast cubes on top and ladle a second cup of the braising liquid over them. At this point, you must be careful of the temperature of the braising liquid—it should feel slightly cool to the touch but not be cold enough to set. If it's too hot, it will melt the layer underneath. Spread another third of the shredded leg meat, while the second cup of liquid hasn't yet set, and ladle another cup of the liquid parsley mixture over it. Let set, then sprinkle with the rest of the duck breast cubes. Ladle ½ cup of the parsley liquid over that and sprinkle with the rest of the shredded

BELOW, LEFT TO RIGHT: *1. Layer terrine.*
Here cubes of cooked duck breast are added.
2. Ladle over clear broth with parsley.
3. Add layer of shredded duck leg meat.

leg meat. Ladle the rest of the braising liquid over the top, and let the terrine set in the refrigerator for at least 8 hours.

When you're ready to serve, run a knife around the sides, flush against the inner wall of the mold. Place a long tray on top of the terrine, hold the mold up against the tray, and turn over the whole assembly, quickly shaking the terrine loose. If the terrine doesn't pop out of the mold, set the mold in a bowl of hot water for about 20 seconds and try again. Slice the terrine with a very sharp, long, thin knife. Don't push down on the terrine as you slice, just move the knife gently back and forth. If you use too much pressure, the terrine slices may break apart (see Slicing Fragile Terrines, below). Serve with cornichons, pickled pearl onions, and Dijon or whole-grain mustard, as desired.

ABOVE, CONTINUED FROM PREVIOUS PAGE:
4. Unmold chilled terrine. 5. Slice terrine very gently with a long sharp knife, or freeze it and slice it with a bread knife as described in Slicing Fragile Terrines at right. 6. A slice of terrine garnished with cornichons and a pickled pearl onion.

Slicing Fragile Terrines

Many of the best terrines are made by suspending tasty solids, such as cubes of duck breast, artichokes, truffles, and prosciutto in a natural jelly, much like a cold consommé, made from meat. The problem is that this jelly must be delicate or it will feel rubbery in the mouth, but if it's too fragile, the terrine will fall apart when you try to slice it. One solution is to make single-serving terrines in individual molds. Another is to freeze a large terrine, slice it with a serrated bread knife while it's still frozen, and then let the slices thaw on the plates in the refrigerator.

Duck Liver Mousse

*T*his simple and inexpensive mousse has a delicious full flavor (but not an aggressive one) and a delicate creaminess that makes it reminiscent of foie gras mousse. The trick behind this mousse is to sauté the livers in hot fat, add a mixture of flavorful ingredients—shallots, herbs, and garlic—to the still-hot pan, and then purée the duck and seasonings with an equal amount of butter, which gives it a silky texture. To further lighten the mousse, I fold in whipped cream. Serve this mousse with toasted slices of country bread. You may have to save up the duck livers in the freezer to accumulate the requisite amount.

MAKES 4 CUPS, ENOUGH FOR 8 FIRST-COURSE SERVINGS OR 15 HORS D'OEUVRES

¾ pound duck livers, trimmed of any small
   threadlike blood vessels and fat
2 tablespoons olive oil
Salt and pepper
2 medium shallots, peeled and chopped fine
1 small clove garlic, peeled and chopped fine
½ teaspoon finely chopped fresh thyme or marjoram, or
   ¼ teaspoon dried thyme or marjoram
¼ cup port, semi-dry Madeira, or cream sherry
2 tablespoons cognac (optional)
½ pound (2 sticks) unsalted butter, plus ¼ pound unsalted butter
1 cup cold heavy cream

Rinse and drain the livers and pat them dry. In a sauté pan or skillet just large enough to hold the livers in a single layer, heat the oil over high heat until it begins to smoke. (It's essential that the pan be very hot or the livers won't brown; instead they will release liquid and end up simmering in their own juices.) Season the livers with salt and pepper to taste and lower them, one by one, into the hot skillet—stand back because duck livers tend to spatter. Brown the livers for about 3 minutes on each side, until they just begin to feel firm to the touch. Use a slotted spoon to scoop them out of the pan and into a bowl.

Pour the cooked fat out of the pan and discard it. While the pan is still hot, use a wooden spoon to stir in the shallots, garlic, and thyme or marjoram—stir them around in the pan for about a minute until they release their fragrance—and pour in the port. Boil the port until it's reduced by about half, add the cognac, if using, boiling it for about 10 seconds, and pour the mixture over the livers. Let the livers cool for 10 minutes.

Cut the ½ pound butter into about six chunks and put these in the bowl with the livers. Let sit for about

15 minutes, allowing the livers to cool and the butter to soften slightly. (Don't, however, let the butter actually melt or it will make the mixture heavy.) Puree the liver-butter mixture in a food processor until smooth, then work it through a drum sieve (a large circular device with a screen stretched over it) or large strainer, using the back of a large spoon or ladle. (Since livers don't have a muscle structure like meat, they will go easily through the strainer.) Season the mixture to taste with salt and pepper.

Make sure the cream is well chilled, then beat it into medium peaks—not too stiff or the mixture will be dry—and quickly whisk one-fourth of the cream into the liver mixture. Fold the liver mixture in with the rest of the cream and season again to taste with salt and pepper. Cover the mousse with plastic wrap, making sure the plastic is pressed against the surface of the mousse (if allowed contact with air, the mousse will turn dark), and chill for at least 3 hours or overnight.

You can serve duck liver mousse in individual ramekins—cover with a layer of melted butter and let it set to form a protective seal, or cover with plastic wrap until you're ready to serve. Use two spoons, facing in the opposite direction, to spoon the mousse out into egg shapes. Arrange two of the "eggs" on each chilled serving plate.

Sources

Asian Ingredients

The CMC Company
P.O. Box 322
Avalon, NJ 08202
800-262-2780
www.thecmccompany.com

The Ethnic Grocer
866-438-4642
www.ethnicgrocer.com

Katagiri
224 East Fifty-ninth Street
New York, NY 10022
212-755-3566
212-752-4197 (fax)
www.katagiri.com

The Oriental Pantry
423 Great Road
Acton, MA 01720
800-828-0368
www.orientalpantry.com

Spice Merchant
P.O. Box 524
Jackson Hole, WY 83001
800-551-5999
www.orientalcookingsecrets.com

Concentrated Stocks and Glazes

More-than-Gourmet
929 Home Avenue
Akron, OH 44310
800-860-9385
www.morethangourmet.com

Dried Chiles

The Chile Shop
109 East Water Street
Santa Fe, NM 87501
505-983-6080
505-984-0737 (fax)
www.thechileshop.com

Kitchen/Market
218 Eighth Avenue
New York, NY 10011
888-HOT-4433
www.kitchenmarket.com

Duck

D'Artagnan
c/o The Golden Egg
(fresh ducks and raw foie gras;
duck confit, fat, and sausages)
www.the-golden-egg.com

Nut Oils

Dean & Deluca
560 Broadway
New York, NY 10012
877-826-9246
800-781-4050 (fax)
www.deandeluca.com

Rosenthal Wine Merchants, Ltd.
1219 Route 83
Shekomeko, NY 12567
800-910-1990
518-398-5974 (fax)
www.madrose.com/home2.html

Smoking Supplies

The Sausage Maker, Inc.
(smokers, sausage makers,
casings, woodchips)
1500 Clinton Street,
Building 123
Buffalo, NY 14206
888-490-8525
716-824-6465 (fax)
www.sausagemaker.com

Broadway Panhandler
(woodchips)
477 Broome Street
New York, NY 10013
866-COOKWARE
www.broadwaypanhandler.com

Wild Mushrooms

Marché aux Delices
(dried and fresh)
888-547-5471
www.auxdelices.com

Urbani USA
(fresh, dried, and frozen)
29–24 Fortieth Avenue
Long Island City, NY 11101
800-281-2330
www.urbani.com

Conversion Charts

WEIGHT EQUIVALENTS

The metric weights given in this chart are not exact equivalents, but have been rounded up or down slightly to make measuring easier.

Avoirdupois	Metric
¼ oz	7 g
½ oz	15 g
1 oz	30 g
2 oz	60 g
3 oz	90 g
4 oz	115 g
5 oz	150 g
6 oz	175 g
7 oz	200 g
8 oz (½ lb)	225 g
9 oz	250 g
10 oz	300 g
11 oz	325 g
12 oz	350 g
13 oz	375 g
14 oz	400 g
15 oz	425 g
16 oz (1 lb)	450 g
1½ lb	750 g
2 lb	900 g
2¼ lb	1 kg
3 lb	1.4 kg
4 lb	1.8 kg

VOLUME EQUIVALENTS

These are not exact equivalents for American cups and spoons, but have been rounded up or down slightly to make measuring easier.

American	Metric	Imperial
¼ t	1.2 ml	
½ t	2.5 ml	
1 t	5.0 ml	
½ T (1.5 t)	7.5 ml	
1 T (3 t)	15 ml	
¼ cup (4 T)	60 ml	2 fl oz
⅓ cup (5 T)	75 ml	2½ fl oz
½ cup (8 T)	125 ml	4 fl oz
⅔ cup (10 T)	150 ml	5 fl oz
¾ cup (12 T)	175 ml	6 fl oz
1 cup (16 T)	250 ml	8 fl oz
1¼ cups	300 ml	10 fl oz (½ pt)
1½ cups	350 ml	12 fl oz
2 cups (1 pint)	500 ml	16 fl oz
2½ cups	625 ml	20 fl oz (1 pint)
1 quart	1 liter	32 fl oz

OVEN TEMPERATURE EQUIVALENTS

Oven Mark	F	C	Gas
Very cool	250–275	130–140	½–1
Cool	300	150	2
Warm	325	170	3
Moderate	350	180	4
Moderately hot	375	190	5
	400	200	6
Hot	425	220	7
	450	230	8
Very hot	475	250	9

Index

BABY BEAR, BABY BEAR, DO YOU SEE?

By Bill Martin Jr
Pictures by Eric Carle

Henry Holt and Company · New York

Baby Bear,
Baby Bear,
what do you see?

I see a red fox
slipping by me.

Red Fox,
Red Fox,
what do you see?

I see a flying squirrel gliding by me.

Flying Squirrel,
Flying Squirrel,
what do you see?

I see a mountain goat
climbing near me.

Mountain Goat,
Mountain Goat,
what do you see?

I see a blue heron
flying by me.

Blue Heron,
Blue Heron,
what do you see?

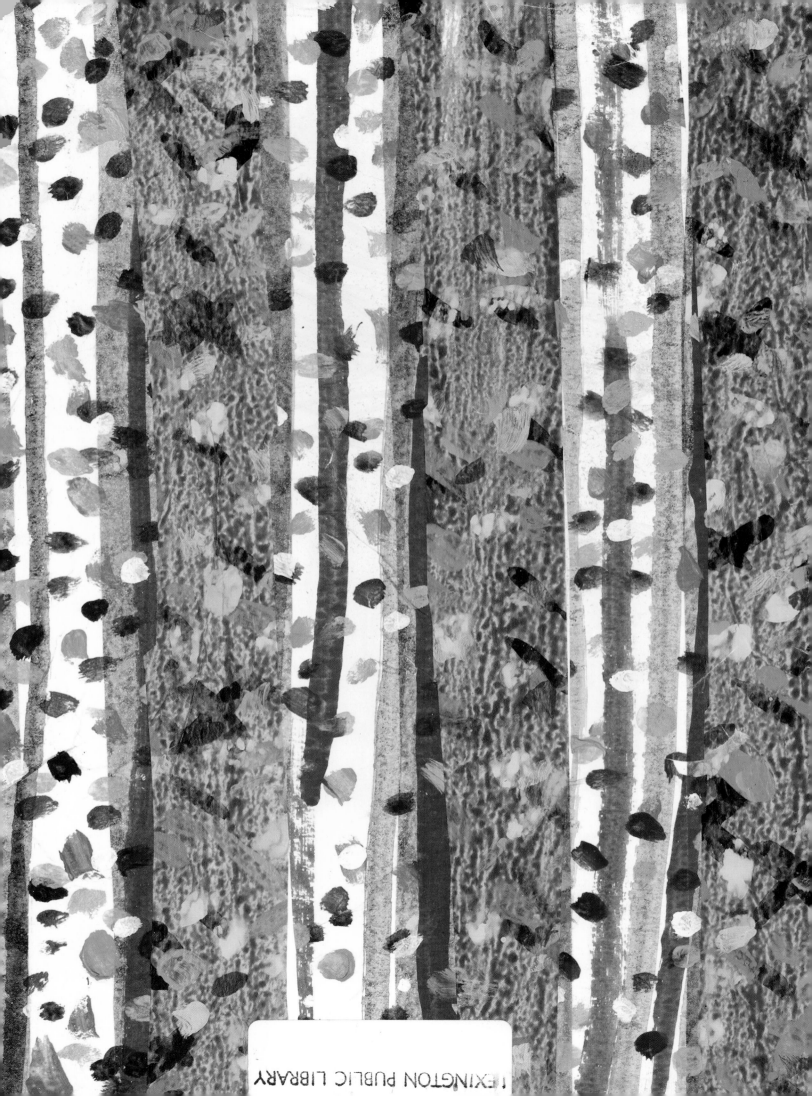

Author's Note

North America is filled with thousands of species of wildlife. These creatures have lived in their habitats for centuries. Together, we can work to ensure that they will remain wild and free forever. This book features ten of these great American animals.

The author wishes to thank Michael Sampson for his help in the preparation of this text.

The Eric Carle Museum of Picture Book Art was built to celebrate the art that we are first exposed to as children. Located in Amherst, Massachusetts, the 40,000-square-foot museum is the first in this country devoted to national and international picture book art.

To learn more about the Eric Carle Museum of Picture Book Art, please visit carlemuseum.org.

To learn more about Eric Carle and his books and products, please visit eric-carle.com.

Henry Holt and Company, LLC
Publishers since 1866
175 Fifth Avenue
New York, New York 10010
mackids.com

Library of Congress Cataloging-in-Publication Data
Martin, Bill, 1916–2004.
Baby bear, baby bear, what do you see? / by Bill Martin Jr ; pictures by Eric Carle.
Summary: Illustrations and rhyming text portray a young bear searching for its mother and meeting many North American animals along the way.
ISBN 978-1-62779-731-3
[1. Bears—Fiction. 2. Mother and child—Fiction. 3. Animals—North America—Fiction.]
I. Carle, Eric, ill. II. Title.
PZ8.3.M418Bab 2007   [E]—dc22   200637769

First edition—2007
10th anniversary edition with audio CD—2016

Printed in China by RR Donnelley Asia Printing Solutions Ltd.,
Dongguan City, Guangdong Province
10 9 8 7 6 5 4 3 2 1

I see a prairie dog
digging by me.

Prairie Dog,
Prairie Dog,
what do you see?

I see a striped skunk
strutting by me.

Striped Skunk,
Striped Skunk,
what do you see?

I see a mule deer running by me.

Mule Deer,
Mule Deer,
what do you see?

I see a rattlesnake
sliding by me.

Rattlesnake,
Rattlesnake,
what do you see?

I see a screech owl
hooting at me.

Screech Owl,
Screech Owl,
what do you see?

I see a mama bear
looking at me.

Mama Bear,
Mama Bear,
what do you see?

I see . . .

a red fox,

a flying squirrel,

a prairie dog,

a striped skunk,

a screech owl and . . .

a mountain goat,   a blue heron,

a mule deer,   a rattlesnake,

**my baby bear
looking at me—
that's what I see!**